BEATING THE
Marriage Odds

BEATING THE
Marriage Odds

By William R. Campbell

Bill Campbell

VMI Publishers
Sisters, Oregon

Beating the Marriage Odds
© 2009 William R. Campbell

All rights reserved
Published by
VMI Publishers
Sisters, Oregon
www.vmipublishers.com

ISBN: 1-935265-03-2
ISBN: 978-1-935265-03-0
Library of Congress: 2009936130

Printed in the USA

Cover design by Joe Bailen

TABLE OF CONTENTS

INTRODUCTION

Most people would not even buy a new car if the dealer told them it had a fifty-percent chance of being a lemon. Yet those are the very same odds we face for a successful marriage. More than half of all marriages today will fail (that's *all* marriages—Christian and non-Christian alike). And, surprisingly, second marriages don't fare any better. In fact, they do considerably worse. More than seventy-five percent of second marriages fail. The statistics are even worse for third marriages, with better than eighty-five percent of third marriages ending in divorce.

Since both my wife and I had experienced the pains of failed marriages, God has given us a passion for trying to help keep others from suffering similar resultant pains and tribulations.

As a pastor, I have performed many wedding ceremonies and have counseled still others contemplating marriage. While working on my master's degree, I learned that couples who undergo some form of premarital counseling do much better than those who do not. This book is, of course, focused on individuals who are engaged or contemplating marriage. It can also minister to couples who never had any significant counseling before marriage or who perhaps received some counseling but have forgotten it. This book may also have application for anyone currently struggling in a relationship.

In seminary I was surprised to learn that a master of divinity degree required only one three-hour counseling course. Experience has taught me this could severely limit the performance of one's pastoral duties. Discussions with other pastors, especially in smaller churches, indicate many lack a sound outline for conducting premarital counseling. *Beating the Marriage Odds*, therefore, has also been designed to serve as a resource and an outline for anyone who does premarital counseling.

All too often I have been called to counsel couples who find themselves in the midst of a crumbling relationship. They had never examined significant red flags to a successful relationship or never discussed expectations about such important matters as whether the wife would work outside the home, whose career would take precedence should one require a move to another city or state, or whether or not the family would attend church, etc. All these issues, along with many others, are best addressed before entering into a "'til death do us part" relationship.

As an aid to those who do premarital counseling, I have included an excellent outline of premarital counseling from a marriage counseling course I had in seminary, plus a few additional topics, which experience has shown to be helpful. This is by no means a complete list; however, it represents a good starting point. Wherever possible, I have used examples to clarify and illustrate points important to a successful relationship.

Jay Carty is a former professional basketball player and founder of Yes! Ministries, an organization dedicated to helping people say "yes!" to God. In his book *Playing with Fire: Do Nice People Really Go to Hell?* Carty shares the following insight from his father, who had been a professional gambler: "Professional gamblers don't bet too much on a long shot. Long-shot gamblers are losers." In other words, professional gamblers make their living by playing the odds.

The principles set forth in this book are directed at improving the odds for a successful and fulfilling marriage. Like vitamins, the fifteen principles presented will do no one any good unless they are accepted, internalized, and digested. Some are based in biblical wisdom; still others are found in secular thought. All represent keys to a stronger, healthier marriage and will only work if consistently and diligently applied.

Because I want people from all backgrounds to benefit from these principles wherever possible, I have tried to restate each biblical principle in terms of a secular parallel. For example, one of my father's earliest teachings was, "If you can't say something good about someone, don't say anything at all." I have tried to practice this principle throughout my life. When I became a Christian, I discovered the biblical origin and parallel to that thought while reading Ephesians 4:29: "Do not let any unwholesome talk come out of your mouths, but only what is helpful for building others up according to their needs, that it may benefit those who listen." This thought has no less value for the non-Christian than for the Christian. To share another example, the biblical command, "Do not commit adultery" does not render adultery any more or less destructive to the Christian marriage than to the marriage of an atheist, a Jew, or a Muslim.

In his book *Quiet Strength: The Principles, Practices, & Priorities of a Winning Life*, author Tony Dungy points to the important role the application of consistent core values and principles has played in his success, both as a coach and as a family man. Applying consistent values and principles in a marriage relationship will likewise help beat the marriage odds.

My goal is to present these principles in ways that are both clear and understandable so marriages might be strengthened and improved through their application. My prayer is that in the process some valuable seeds might be planted, or that seeds already planted might be watered, keeping ever mindful that God alone causes the growth.

The poet Robert Burns once wrote, "Oh what a gift that God could give us, to see ourselves as others see us." God has given me that gift, and her name is Phyllis. This book is dedicated to Phyllis—my wife, my best friend, my companion, and my lover—she is all these things and much more.

I recently heard a message from a pastor during which he quoted pastor and Bible teacher Adrian Rogers, who proclaimed his wife was his best friend. So much so, in fact, "that if she ever leaves me," he said, "I'm going with her." This statement might well sum up one of the major goals of this book—that we might all feel this same closeness in our own marriage relationships.

Chapter 1

Things to Consider Before You Say
"'Til Death Do Us Part!"

My wife and I usually begin premarital counseling with a couple by watching and discussing the film *I Do: Portraits From Our Journey* (available from the Family Research Council). Thus, I can think of no better way to begin this book than to review and examine closely the marriage vows. After all, a "'til death do us part" promise before a holy God is best not taken lightly.

The video and this chapter both examine each of the vows (giving examples how that vow might play itself out in a real-life marriage). These examples, as with most of the examples in this book, have been taken from actual couples. Names have been changed to protect the privacy of those individuals involved.

The purpose of taking such a close look at these marriage vows is to assure they are regarded with the respect and consideration due them. After all, the decision to marry is one of the most important decisions most of us will make in our entire lifetime. Thus, the vows should be more than mere words recited by rote. We will examine each vow with a view toward a richer understanding of the commitment being made to one another.

Perhaps nothing is more discouraging for a pastor or priest who has asked couples to recite these words from *The Book of Common Prayer:* "I, _____, take you, _____, to be my wedded (wife/husband); to have and to hold from this day forward, for better or for worse, for richer for poorer, in sickness and in health, to love and to cherish, 'til death do us part, according to God's holy ordinance; and therefore I pledge you my love;" and then find out months or years down the road the couple has divorced.

Let's examine the word "vow" as defined in *Webster's Encyclopedic Dictionary:* "a solemn promise; an engagement solemnly entered into; an oath made to God or to some deity to perform some act on the performance of certain conditions; to promise solemnly to give, consecrate, or dedicate by a solemn promise, as to a divine power."

The problem is not a simple one. We all make promises with the full intention of keeping them. It is only later, when we break a vow, that we make excuses. "It's not my fault," we say. "He/she is just too difficult to live with." Or, "I simply cannot forgive what he/she has done." Or one I hear frequently: "Surely God would want me to be happy!" This last excuse reminds me of Adam's response after sinning: "The woman you gave me told me to eat it." In other words, it was God's fault in the first place.

Excusing wrongful behavior in no way makes such behavior right. We can all come up with dozens of reasons to get out of something we've committed to. The vows to marry, however, are vows not only to our spouse, but to God. There is a reason the president of the United States and others holding office in this country or testifying before a court of law are asked to place their hand on the Bible as an implication they are making a commitment before God. It is always less convicting to commit ourselves to a person than to a holy God.

TO HAVE AND TO HOLD

Let's examine the words of the marriage vow more closely. First, let's take a look at perhaps the least difficult of all the marriage vows, "to have and to hold." I recommend the book *The Five Love Languages:*

How to Express Heartfelt Commitment to Your Mate by Dr. Gary Chapman. This book details five different ways people express love to one another. One of those ways is *physical touch*. Some of us were raised in homes with lots of hugging and kissing. To others, such open display of affection makes them feel uncomfortable or, in some extreme cases, even unwelcome. Frequently couples do not share the same love language. One may crave *physical touch*, while the other may want one of the other four love languages: *words of affirmation, acts of service, receiving gifts,* or *quality time.* Our natural tendency is to give to others what we ourselves desire. Problems often arise when we speak a different love language than our partner.

For example, a friend of mine, Tim, desires lots of hugging, hand holding, and other public displays of affection. His wife, Ann, feels loved when Tim comes home early from work and spends quality time with her. Since each has a different need, it is important to recognize the tendency to do for others what we ourselves like. Therefore, it is possible neither Tim nor Ann is getting their emotional needs met. Ann must step out of her comfort zone and engage in public displays of love that may, at times, feel uncomfortable to her. Tim must likewise recognize his wife's needs are different. She feels loved when he makes an effort to spend quality time with her. This will require both Tim and Ann to expend extra effort to meet the other's needs.

Usually we will each have more than just one such need. Discovering our partner's needs and meeting them is a key to having a happy and fulfilling relationship. If we don't know what their needs are, we must ask them. Studying *The Five Love Languages* together will help us better understand our love needs as well as our spouse's.

FOR BETTER OR FOR WORSE

Next, let us study: "for better or for worse." Obviously most of us are quite comfortable with the "better," but what about "for worse"?

Bob and Julie were married for only a short time when Bob became suspicious of Julie. She was not only required to work late on occasion, but also seemed to be enjoying her work more than he thought she should. When Julie announced she was pregnant, Bob immediately suspected she had a lover at work. They fought, and eventually separated. Bob's father had abandoned his mother, leaving her to raise their children as a single parent, and Bob had sworn he would never be such a father. Yet, now, he found himself in just such a situation. Fortunately, Bob realized his error, returned to his wife and child, and they began a new relationship—one based on trust and responsibility.

Another couple, Ellen and Andrew, were married only a short while when Andrew was laid off. Unable to either obtain a new job or to qualify for unemployment, and with Ellen pregnant and unable to work, they found themselves homeless. The stress led to constant fights, which eventually led to a separation. For a time, Ellen moved back in with her parents, while Andrew continued to unsuccessfully seek employment in their small town. Eventually Ellen sought counseling, reunited with Andrew, and they were encouraged to explore an option they had not considered (a move to a larger city with greater opportunity for Andrew to find suitable employment). Andrew went ahead, found a new job, and Ellen soon followed.

Such circumstances, repeat themselves daily, both in our local communities and all across this country. Stress, like frustration, often leads to anger, and can then lead to the deterioration of relationships.

Life is not easy, nor does Scripture tell us it will be; quite the contrary. The Bible records these words of Jesus in John 16:33, "In this life you will have troubles." So, before marrying, each person should ponder this: What will I do when trouble comes? Not if, but when trouble comes. Prepare mentally for the difficult times to come. Don't assume that happiness is a constant. We cannot plan for every eventuality, but the better we prepare mentally for the "what ifs," the better we will react in difficult situations.

FOR RICHER FOR POORER

The next vow is "for richer for poorer." On the surface we might think the "for richer" part would not be a problem, but don't judge too quickly. I have seen many couples' relationships destroyed by an unexpected inheritance or winning the lottery. This seems like an event that should solve problems rather than cause them, but, for many, the unexpected acquisition of wealth can be a very real problem.

We have heard some of the horror stories of people who have won the lottery and subsequently been alienated from family and friends, or even divorced as a result of issues arising out of this newfound wealth.

Consider a couple, Rita and Tom, who both worked outside the home and lived quite comfortably on their salaries. Rita's parents were killed in a plane crash, and she inherited a substantial sum of money. She quit her job and, perhaps to stem the tremendous depression she was feeling, began to spend money in extravagant ways. When Tom questioned the wisdom of her expenditures, she became angry, then hostile, and eventually they separated. How could this have happened? The expression "easy come, easy go" would seem to apply in this case. Money suddenly acquired, through no effort of our own, seems to be less valued by the recipient. If one partner values savings more than another, it will amplify such problems in a relationship. (See Chapter VII, "Finances," for more information on this subject.)

Poverty is, of course, an unwelcome guest in any home. This aspect of the "for richer for poorer" vow is much easier to relate to for most of us. Generally speaking, the lack of funds is more stressful to relationships than an excess of funds. Finances are the second leading cause of marital breakups. Stress comes into play in such situations.

Issues to consider before marriage include: How would we handle the loss of a job and resultant loss of income? Are my partner's views on money compatible with my own (i.e. is he/she a spender, and I a saver)? Am I more ambitious than my partner? Do we have a backup plan in the event of a financial setback? In all of these instances, looking ahead and trying to anticipate difficulties almost always reduces the impact of problems down the road. Some of these questions relate to expectations. (See Chapter IX on "Mind Games" and the section on expectations for further understanding.) While similar to the "for better or for worse" section in many regards, this vow speaks exclusively to financial issues. In summary: Expect financial problems; anticipate and plan for them in order to be prepared when they occur.

IN SICKNESS AND IN HEALTH

The vow, "In sickness and in health," sounds harmless enough on the surface, and yet these simple words hold the potential for devastation down the road unless we truly take them to heart. When we get married, many of us are young and healthy and feel like we are going to live forever. This can quickly change.

Let's first consider a couple in their early twenties, married for just over one year. The wife is involved in a car accident and is rendered a paraplegic for the rest of her life. One day this couple's life was normal; the next their world was turned upside down.

How would you react in such a situation? One day, your only thoughts are of family, friends, work, and, perhaps, what to do with your free time on the upcoming weekend. Most of us take life and health for granted. Then, suddenly, everything changes; you find yourself a full-time caregiver, assisting your spouse to do the most elemental things—eating, bathing, getting dressed, and so forth. If this is what "in sickness and in health" might mean, ask yourself, "Am I prepared for that level of commitment?"

The book *Scarred*, by Dave Roever, provides another insight into this commitment. While serving in Vietnam, Dave had a phosphorous grenade explode in his hand, leaving him badly injured and disfigured for life. He tells of lying in his hospital bed next to another badly burned vet. The wife of the other patient appeared one day, took off her wedding ring, tossed it between her husband's charred feet, and stated, "You're embarrassing. I couldn't walk down the street with you." Then she walked out. Imagine how devastating this was for the young soldier and for Dave, who for days after feared how his own wife might react to his scars. He needn't have worried, however. His wife loved him for who he was—not for what he looked like. Ask yourself if you could see past the scars to the person inside.

Or consider the possibility of your spouse coming home with the news he/she has terminal cancer and perhaps less than a year to live, or the diagnosis of multiple sclerosis or some other degenerative disease. Later in life, many are afflicted with Alzheimer's disease. Some individuals find life at this point too difficult to deal with and either abandon their spouses or relegate them to a nursing home. I'm not trying to be morose, just seeking understanding of the true meaning of remaining committed "in sickness and in health."

I know couples who are living out such circumstances. Some to the glory of God, and others who have abandoned their spouses at a time of their greatest need. Ask yourself honestly how you would deal with an unexpected serious illness. Consider a worst-case scenario. These are difficult questions to answer, and even to ask. They may seem far-fetched; however, resist the temptation to dismiss them. Rather, having asked them, contemplate whether you are ready for the commitment of marriage and all it means.

TO LOVE AND TO CHERISH

The marriage vow "to love and to cherish" also deals with commitment. Many ceremonies use the words "to love, honor, and obey." While this concept seems to some offensive or perhaps not "politically correct," I always give couples their choice of preferred wording here. The biblical concept of the wife submitting to, or being obedient to, her husband and the concept of the man being the "head of the wife" is often misinterpreted. In context this means the wife is to submit to the husband just as she submits to the Lord. And the husband is to be the head of his wife as Christ is head of the church. This refers simply to submitting ourselves to God's order of things. Wives submit to husbands; children submit to parents; workers submit to employers. It is worth noting in the biblical account of the creation of a "helper suitable for him" that Eve was not taken from Adam's head that she would be over him, or from his feet that she would be under him, but rather from his side that she would walk beside him as a companion and a helpmate.

Just as with governments, we are called to submit to God's appointed authority, unless to do so would mean to deny the Lord. Without authority and without submission, we have only anarchy. But with all authority comes responsibility. For example, though my wife is called to respect my authority, it is my responsibility to earn that respect by being a loving husband, a spiritual leader in my home, and by not abusing the authority I have been given.

It is important to understand that submission in the biblical sense never implies or carries with it the idea of inferiority. Jesus submits to God, but He is not inferior to God. Neither is the woman inferior to man. In submitting to her husband, the wife is submitting to the Lord. Such an understanding of God's idea of and purpose for submission will usually aid in the understanding and application of this biblical passage.

This is one of the most misunderstood and abused passages of Scripture. It is no more appropriate for a man to beat his chest and parade around the house demanding, "Do as I say woman!" than it is for a wife to boss her husband around, thus usurping the authority God has given him. Respect and balance are required by both the husband and the wife. And, as I have often reminded my children, "Respect can neither be legislated nor demanded, only earned."

'TIL DEATH DO US PART

The last words of the vows, "'til death do us part," are rightly related to death, since death represents the end of our earthly lives. Jesus said in Matthew 19:6, "What God has joined together, let man not separate." (See also, Chapter III, "The 'D' Word.") We are intended by God to be married until one of us dies. This should be the only ending to a marriage.

This commitment is so serious that you are pledging to your spouse and to God you will remain married through all sorts of trials and tribulations until death, and death alone, separates you. As my own father said to me when I announced my engagement many years ago, "Don't take this commitment lightly; you'll be married for the rest of your life." That is, in fact, God's plan, and it should be ours!

Neither good times nor bad, neither sickness nor health, neither wealth nor poverty, nor any other affliction known to man can rightly be used as a justification for breaking the bonds of matrimony. This applies to everyone, whether you've been married for years or are just now about to enter a marriage relationship.

So then, what principle would best be extracted from this chapter? What principle, if adhered to or applied to your life, might improve your chances of beating the marriage odds?

> ## PRINCIPLE:
> **Consider, and take to heart, every aspect of the marriage vows before making a "'til death do us part" solemn promise to God and to your spouse.**

BIBLICAL VERSES ON VOWS

Numbers 30:1–2 "Moses said …: 'This is what the LORD commands: When a man makes a vow to the LORD or takes an oath to obligate himself by a pledge, he must not break his word but must do everything he said.'"

These verses make it clear that the Lord takes seriously those things we promise to Him.

Ecclesiastes 8:2 "Obey the King's command, I say, because you took an oath before God."

This would apply to the marriage vows, which are by definition an oath before God.

Psalm 119:105–106 "Your word is a lamp to my feet and a light for my path. I have taken an oath and confirmed it, that I will follow your righteous laws."

These verses point to the light of God's Word, which guides us, and to the determination and commitment to obey God's words that we and others might be blessed.

Matthew 5:33, 37 "Again, you have heard that it was said to the people long ago, 'Do not break your oath, but keep the oaths you have made to the Lord.' Simply let your 'Yes' be 'Yes,' and your 'No' be ' No' ..."

These verses, spoken by Jesus were used to counsel us not to swear falsely before the Lord. For the Christian it indicates our word can be taken to mean what we say, since we are to speak the truth. God has said to lie would be a sin.

Chapter II

THE MARRIAGE MYTH

Many couples' view of marriage is as much a cause of marital failure as is a basic lack of understanding of the institution and the very nature of the marriage relationship. Many people think of marriage as a contractual relationship between a man and a woman. We see this evidenced by the surge in prenuptial agreements. A prenuptial contract is, by its very nature, a fallback plan in case the marriage doesn't work out.

It is common for couples contemplating marriage to approach it with the idea that failure of the marriage is possible or, in some cases, even probable. I have talked with couples who believed that if their marriage didn't work out, divorce was always an option. Yet, in most instances during the premarital counseling phase, couples reject the idea of their own marriage failing. "That will never happen to us," seems to be their prevailing sentiment. Couples in love frequently assume divorce is simply something that happens to other people.

Why do so many marriages today fail? I believe the view of marriage as a contract is part of the problem. Compare a contractual view of marriage with God's view of marriage: a covenant relationship between God, a husband, and a wife. Let me point out how this covenant relationship should work when properly applied. This covenant relationship involves a three-way promise.

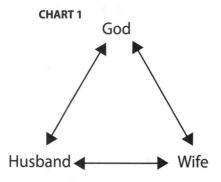

CHART 1

Both parties make a promise to each other and to God. These promises should not be taken lightly. For this promise to have effect, the couple must revere God. If the couple views God as sovereign they will not take lightly a promise made to Him. The wisdom of the words of King Solomon in Ecclesiastes 4:12 should be obvious to Christian and non-Christian alike: "Though one may be overpowered, two can defend themselves. A cord of three strands is not quickly broken." This "cord of three strands" is for Christians a picture of two people growing closer to each other daily as they each grow closer to God.

A braid appears to contain only two strands of hair. But it is impossible to create a braid with only two strands. If the two could be put together at all, they would quickly unravel. Herein lies the mystery: What looks like two strands requires a third. The third strand, though not immediately evident, keeps the strands tightly woven. In a Christian marriage, God's presence, like the third strand in a braid, holds husband and wife together.

My wife and I seem to grow closer together with each passing day, yet both of us agree this is not through any super-human effort on either of our parts. Rather, we become closer because we both are daily looking to Jesus' example of perfection. This example is far better than we could conceive through any construction of our own. Compare this with a contractual relationship in which the strains and stresses of jobs, educational training, and friendships can inevitably cause couples to grow apart and say, "I don't want to be married to you anymore."

For years, couples have repeated these words: "For better or for worse, in sickness or in health, for richer or poorer, 'til death do us part." These words are then followed by the minister's admonition, "For what God has joined together, let man not separate." The words seem to have meaning at the time they are repeated, yet are easily forgotten in times of trouble in the marriage.

Perhaps one of the biggest mistakes couples make is buying into the popular myth that marriage is a fifty-fifty proposition. To enter into a marriage relationship with this view is to build the marriage on a faulty foundation. Living out the marriage relationship with the philosophy "I'll do my part, you do yours" will most likely doom the relationship from its inception. Note I am not talking here about the two-way contractual relationship mentioned earlier, rather I am speaking of the *degree of effort* put forth by each of the marriage partners.

For a marriage to succeed, each party must attempt to give 100 percent to the relationship. I say attempt, because I don't think any of us is actually capable of such an effort. However, aiming for 100 percent will get a person close enough to achieve a successful relationship.

Let me give an illustration from a speech class I once took. The speech teacher told soft-spoken students to "shout" and loud students to "whisper" while making their speeches. When the soft-spoken students thought they were shouting, they were actually much closer to a normal range of speaking. The opposite was true for the loud students when they whispered. This illustrates giving 100 percent to a relationship. Though I might *think* I give in to my wife 100 percent of the time, the reality is something less than that.

An excellent book by Drs. Les and Leslie Parrott, *Saving Your Marriage Before It Starts: Seven Questions to Ask Before (and After) You*

Marry, discusses several other marriage myths. In this book, the Parrotts point out one of the most common and harmful myths couples believe is that both partners expect exactly the same things from marriage. However, because of our diverse upbringings, backgrounds, varying role expectations, and many unconscious rules for living, this is seldom the case. For this reason, in counseling I spend a great deal of time prior to marriage discussing each partner's expectations. (These are further elaborated in Chapter IX "Mind Games.")

Two additional myths exposed in the book are that "everything good in the relationship will get better, and everything bad will disappear." The reality is the good things that first attracted us to our mates often can later become irritants.

For example, there is a flip side to everything. A couple came to us for counseling with the following complaints: When John first met Marsha, he saw her as *free spirited* and *whimsical*. After seven years of marriage, these things that first attracted him to Marsha he now saw as *irresponsible* and *thoughtless*. Likewise, what originally attracted Marsha to John was his *decisiveness*. Marsha saw John as *confident*. She now saw him as *overbearing* and *suffocating*. We observe this pattern in relationships quite often and, therefore, always inquire of couples what initially attracted them to their mates.

As to bad things disappearing, *aux contraire*. If something irritates us before marriage, it will only get worse after marriage. Couples frequently come in for counseling and complain about something irritating their spouse does. I always ask, "Were they like that when you married them?" Invariably the answer is, "Yes." I then ask the offended spouses why they expect their partner to be any different now than they were before they married them?

It is important to recognize we cannot change our spouse. Note: This is not the same as saying they *cannot* change. It is saying, rather, that *we* do not have the power to change them. The good and bad we see in our spouse does not disappear after we are married.

Another dangerous myth is: "My spouse will make me whole." Marriage, however, is not a personal growth hormone. To buy into this myth is to become overly dependent and enmeshed. This myth is similar to the myth "My spouse will make me happy." We enter dangerous waters when we look to others for our happiness. Happiness comes from within. Only God has the power to complete us or to make us happy.

For example, during counseling Peter told me he had first been attracted to a coworker because she made him feel happy and wanted, something he said his wife did not do for him. I pointed out that happiness is a choice. We choose to be happy, just as we choose to drive our car or walk to work. Often, people not vested in a relationship can appear attractive to someone like Peter, whose wife was struggling with all the responsibilities of maintaining a home, preparing meals for her family, and taking care of a new baby (including nighttime feedings). I pointed out to Peter it was neither his responsibility to make his wife happy, nor was it her responsibility to make him happy. In marriage, our responsibility to our partner is to love and respect him/her unconditionally. Interestingly enough, this usually makes them happy.

I once heard it said the real test of a man was not when he played the role he wanted for himself but when he played the role destiny had for him. If I were to rephrase that, I would say the real test is not in living out the marriage they always dreamed of, but rather in living out the marriage they are currently in. We are too easily trapped into the "grass is greener" mindset, always looking for something we think will be better. This is perhaps the reason second and third marriages fail at an even greater rate than first marriages.

To experience a healthy marriage, couples must establish a "family nationality" or a "team identity." Husband and wife need to be a team. Joined together, as the vows imply, "For better or for worse, in sickness and in health, for richer or poorer, 'til death do us part!"

Make no mistake, marriage is hard work. Problems do not decrease after marriage; in fact, logic would say they might double. I certainly do not say this to discourage anyone from marriage, but rather to encourage people to face the reality of marriage. Marriage requires two people willing to work together to solve problems. Such an approach minimizes problems, but does not eliminate them.

As stated in the introduction, my wife and I both agree the first principle for this chapter has been, for us, the single most important principle of this book. For most of us, it is difficult to admit to any weakness—usually this is a pride issue. Perhaps that is why Solomon, one of the wisest men of all times, recorded in Proverbs that God, "hates pride" and "pride comes before destruction." Yet the Apostle Paul said that God's grace and power are made perfect in our weakness (2 Corinthians 12:9). So, the question for us would be, "Am I strong enough to admit that I am weak?" Because God gave us free will, we are free to say, " I can do this on my own. I don't need any help." Or, we can say, "I can do all things through Christ who strengthens me!" All of which leads me to the first principle of this chapter. This is the same principle applied by a court of law where people are sworn in with their hand on the Bible.

I am compelled to point out I could find no secular counterpart for this principle. But I make no apology for its inclusion. To disregard it would have been intellectually dishonest of me. I once read that integrity was the pursuit of truth—even if it is other than what we believe.

PRINCIPLE:
For couples who believe in God, a three-way covenant relationship offers greater strength than a mere two-way contractual relationship.

Only two chapters in the book contain more than one principle. However, I consider both of the principles in this chapter to be key to building a successful and lasting marriage relationship.

My father never required a good result; what he did require was a good effort. If we give all we have to something, we can never truly fail. The failure comes only in a failure to give our best effort. Thus the second principle of this chapter:

> **PRINCIPLE:**
> The closer you come to putting 100 percent effort into your marriage, the greater your odds are for a successful marriage.

BIBLICAL VERSES ON MARRIAGE

Genesis 1:27–28 "So God created man in his own image, in the image of God he created him; male and female he created them. God blessed them and said to them, 'Be fruitful and increase in number; fill the earth and subdue it. Rule over the fish of the sea and the birds of the air and over every living creature that moves on the ground.'"

God's purpose in creation is for us to multiply. This can only be accomplished in a heterosexual relationship, as God designed.

Genesis 2:24 "For this reason a man will leave his father and mother and be united to his wife, and they will become one flesh."

This verse refers to the sexual union of man and woman and to the establishment of a new family unit.

Ecclesiastes 4:9–12 "Two are better than one, because they have a good return for their work: If one falls down, his friend can help him up. But pity the man who falls and has no one to help him up! Also, if two lie down together, they will keep warm. But how can one keep warm alone? Though one may be overpowered, two can defend themselves. A cord of three strands is not quickly broken."

This is best understood as reference to a stronger marriage with Christ or God at the center of the relationship.

Hebrews 13:4 "Marriage should be honored by all, and the marriage bed kept pure, for God will judge the adulterer and all the sexually immoral."

In this day, and in an age of rampant sexually transmitted diseases, this reality seems self-evident.

Chapter III

THE "D" WORD

As mentioned in the introduction to this book, my wife and I have each suffered through a divorce. Some may say this would disqualify me to write a book on marriage. My prayer is that others might learn from my mistakes. This is in keeping with the following verses from 2 Corinthians 1:3–4, "Praise be to the God and Father of our Lord Jesus Christ, the Father of compassion and the God of all comfort, who comforts us in all our troubles, *so that we can comfort those in any trouble with the comfort we ourselves have received* from God" (emphasis added).

If we do not learn from our mistakes, we are doomed to repeat them. The verse above truly spoke to my heart; for I pray God might use my life lessons to keep someone else from such mistakes and sufferings.

When I applied to seminary, I was already divorced. As a result of my divorce, I was required to write a paper on what I believed was the biblical position on divorce. As a relatively new Christian, I was forced to open the Scriptures and discover exactly what the Bible said about divorce. (As with other chapters, I have included Scriptures at the conclusion of the chapter that deal specifically with this topic.) After experiencing the effects divorce has on children, relatives, friends, and all concerned, I believe that divorce is not a road anyone should travel. It is painful, financially burdensome, and destructive to the lives of children and all involved. As the Scriptures say, God hates divorce.

To provide an insight to the kind of damage I'm talking about, I've listed some of the responses given by children at a youth gathering. They were asked to complete the sentence beginning with, "I wish ..."

"I wish I had a father."

"I wish I could help my mom with all her problems."

"I wish I didn't feel so unimportant."

"I wish I had two parents."

"I wish I were in a family that had a dad."

"I wish I could turn back time and start over."

"I wish my mom and dad loved each other."

This sampling of comments reveals the kind of pain that inevitably results from divorce. In counseling children of divorced parents I find a number of common reactions. First, the children often harbor guilt feelings. They feel they are somehow responsible for their parents' breakup. Second, they frequently feel guilty for loving their father; as if, by doing so, they are somehow being unfaithful to their mother. The reverse is true as well; they think if they love their mother they are somehow betraying their father.

It is not unusual for children of divorced parents to act out in school, or to withdraw, or to have their grades drop. Other common occurrences are increases in depression, truancy, teen pregnancies, drug and alcohol abuse, and sometimes even suicide.

Having watched our own children wrestle with some of these feelings, and noting that even today scars remain because of our past actions, my wife and I have been forced to take a new, serious look at the marriage commitment and what it means.

As a result of our personal experiences in failed relationships, both my wife and I entered our marriage with the understanding divorce would not be an option for us. We also agreed that the "D" word would never be used in our home. I remember someone asking the wife of Billy Graham if she had ever entertained the idea of divorcing her husband. She jokingly replied, "Divorce … No! Murder … Yes!" Seriously, though, the "D" word should never be introduced or threatened. It is equivalent to planting a seed of destruction in one's mind and in one's marriage.

Before entering a marriage, couples should make a conscious decision that divorce is not an option and vow never to use the word in their home. Once the very word "divorce" is introduced into a home, it is like a weed planted. It will grow against all odds and can destroy a relationship. Any plan conceived with the thought of failure is a plan to fail!

We have become a society of quitters. It's easier to quit the music lessons paid for by Mom or Dad than to quit the lessons we saved so long to afford. It's easy to decide an old car isn't good enough when our best friend just bought a brand new vehicle. So-called "friends" who have experienced failed marriages themselves may even offer advice such as, "You were always too good for him (her)," or say, "I told you so." After all, no one likes being alone in a sinking ship.

True friends are the ones who advise us to stay the course;* they remind us of the qualities that first attracted us to our husband or wife. They suggest counseling, and often point out that marriage is a commitment made to God as well as to our spouse. They also remind us that what is needed is not a change *of* partners, but rather a change *in* partners. Lastly, they remind us God hates divorce.

In a real-life situation we encountered, a counselee we'll call Mandy was having difficulty in her new marriage and returned home to her parents. They were sympathetic and meant well, but having originally advised against the marriage, they took an "I told you so" approach. They encouraged Mandy to leave her new husband. Parents frequently have a built-in bias not helpful in counseling. In such situations, parents frequently neglect to find out what role their own child might have played in the breakup. Lacking objectivity, parents usually listen to a one-sided telling of events, with no inclination to hear the "rest of the story." Well-meaning parents often counsel their children to divorce, not allowing for professional counseling or God to do a work in the

21

relationship. By the time Mandy came in for counseling, she had her mind set on divorce, and, though she seemed open to reconciliation, she was unable to overcome her predisposition to leave her husband.

It is natural and common for parents to be protective of their children, even after they are grown. The biblical admonition to "leave and cleave" is a difficult concept for many families. The closer the family ties, the more difficult it is to leave one's birth family and cleave to one's spouse. It is also difficult for a new partner to enter into such a close-knit family. An adversarial relationship may even develop between the new spouse and the enmeshed family unit. Such families have many qualities to recommend them, but anyone wishing to marry into such a close-knit family must be willing to fully join in or run the risk of being on the outside looking in.

It is important to remember we often seek help from those nearest us. Yet, usually those closest to us are least able to provide the objectivity required for sound advice. In Chapter XIII, "Advice for Troubled Times," many of the reasons typically presented for not seeking counseling are listed along with reasons those arguments may not be valid. Remember, it is best to seek advice from those who are best qualified to give it. If we think we cannot afford counseling or that our problems are not significant enough (both common thoughts for young couples) read Chapter XIII.

PRINCIPLE:

Enter your marriage with the mutual understanding that divorce will not be discussed in your home, nor will it be an option for you (not a change of partners, but a change in the partners).

---

*Do not misunderstand the thought here. When I talk about recommending couples stay together, I am not suggesting that anyone should stay in an "at risk" or an abusive relationship or in any way to place themselves in harm's way. An abusive relationship might involve physical, emotional, and/or verbal abuse. It can also include those relationships involving substance abuse. It is possible, however, that *separation*—rather than divorce—may lead to an awakening on the part of the offending spouse that he or she needs help.

BIBLICAL COMMENTARY ON DIVORCE

Malachi 2:15–16 "Has not the LORD made them one? In flesh and spirit they are his. And why one? Because he was seeking godly offspring. So guard yourself in your spirit, and do not break faith with the wife of your youth. 'I hate divorce,' says the LORD God of Israel …"

God's intent for marriage is clear from these verses—one man and one woman joined together for life.

Old Testament Levitical law, given through Moses, permitted Jewish men to divorce their wives. When the Pharisees asked Jesus about this, His reply is given in **Matthew 19:3–9**:

"Some Pharisees came to him to test him. They asked, 'Is it lawful for a man to divorce his wife for any and every reason?'

'Haven't you read,' he replied, 'that at the beginning the Creator "made them male and female," and said, "For this reason a man will leave his father and mother and be united to his wife, and the two will become one flesh." So they are no longer two, but one. Therefore what God has joined together, let man not separate.'

'Why then,' they asked, 'did Moses command that a man give his wife a certificate of divorce and send her away?'

Jesus replied, 'Moses permitted you to divorce your wives because your hearts were hard. But it was not this way from the beginning. I tell you that anyone who divorces his wife, except for marital unfaithfulness, and marries another that woman commits adultery.'"

Clearly God's plan is for a lifetime union between one man and one woman. That is why the Apostle Paul cautions that marriage is difficult and not for everyone. Marriage is a solemn commitment, not to be taken lightly.

Romans 7: 1–3 "Do you not know, brothers—for I am speaking to men who know the law—that the law has authority over a man only as long as he lives? For example, by law a married woman is bound to her husband as long as he is alive, but if he dies, she is released from the law of marriage. So then, if she marries another man while her husband is still alive, she is called an adulteress. But if her husband dies, she is released from that law and is not an adulteress, even though she marries another man."

This verse makes clear that the death of one of the partners releases the living spouse from the marriage vows and frees them to remarry.

1 Corinthians 7: 10–11 "To the married I give this command (not I, but the Lord): A wife must not separate from her husband. But if she does, she must remain unmarried or else be reconciled to her husband. And a husband must not divorce his wife."

These verses speak to separation as opposed to divorce as an option for the Christian. This would apply in such cases as spousal abuse, child abuse, and substance abuse. God does not want anyone to remain in a high-risk relationship, such as those mentioned. Often separation will serve as a wakeup call for the offending spouse.

Chapter IV

TRUE LOVE

Most of us can remember what we considered our first "true love." As we grow to adulthood, each of these childhood attractions *feel* to us like "true love." Yet, as we mature, we come to recognize we cannot always rely on our feelings. My first "true love" was in third grade. Erica was from Sweden, had blond hair and an accent (a fatal combination at that early age). My next "true love" was during the seventh grade, and that relationship lasted through my freshman year in high school.

The problem with the worldly view of "true love" is that it's usually based on feelings. Most of us think of love as an emotion—especially during puberty. During this time, "falling in lust" is often mistaken for "falling in love."

To make my point more clear, let me share a true story. I was listening to the radio one day and heard a minister from India tell this story: My son came to me one day as he approached his twenty-first birthday and said: "Father, I would like to follow the ways of our country and have you select my bride for me" (a common custom in India).

The father recalled how he reacted to the suggestion. "Son, I do not think that is a good idea." The son, however, was determined and enlisted the aid of an aunt still living in India to select his bride for him. The bride and groom corresponded, set a date, and sent out wedding invitations.

The day finally arrived when he was to pick up his bride-to-be at the airport and meet her for the first time. Wishing his father to be a part of this important day, the young man asked his father to accompany him to the airport. The father agreed and recalled a conversation they had on the way to the airport. "Son," he said, "what if she gets off the plane, looks at you, and says, 'Oh, I hope that is not him!' Or, you look at her and think, 'Oh, I hope that is not her.'"

"My son's response is one I will never forget. He said: 'Father I am only going to say this once. Love is not an emotion; it is a matter of will.' I have thought of that often," said the father. "After all these many years, he is the only one of my children who is still married. All the rest have divorced."

Charles Swindoll wrote: "The longer I live, the more I realize the impact of attitude on life. Attitude, to me, is more important than facts. It is more important than the past, than education, than money, than circumstances, than failures, than successes, than what other people think or say or do. It is more important than appearance, giftedness, or skill. It will make or break a company, a church, a home. The remarkable thing is we have a choice every day regarding the attitude we will embrace for that day. We cannot change our past … we cannot change the fact that people will act in a certain way. We cannot change the inevitable. The only thing we can do is play on the one string we have, and that is our attitude. I am convinced that life is ten percent what happens to me and ninety percent how I react to it. And so it is with you … we are in charge of our attitudes."

We have control over our attitude just as we have control over a decision to love someone. As already stated, *love is a decision—a choice—not simply an emotion.* A marriage based upon feelings is built on a shifting foundation. Most people rely too heavily on their emotions. The problem with emotions is that they can, and do change. The phrase "an emotional roller coaster" gives a picture of what I am talking about. Simply put, the "warm fuzzies" people experience in a dating relationship are insufficient grounds for marriage.

The Greek language contains three different words for the English word translated "love," *eros*, *phileo*, and *agape*.

EROS is sexual love. It is the word from which we derive the English word "erotic."

PHILEO is friendship or brotherly love. This is the word from which our English word "Philadelphia" originates.

AGAPE is the love God has for us. *Agape* is an unconditional and serving love. This kind of sacrificial love is at the heart of a good marriage. It is not dependent on what another person does or says.

In the Bible when men are exhorted to "love" their wives, the Greek word used is *agape*. Women, on the other hand are told to "respect" their husbands. I highly recommend a wonderful book (and video series) that deals with this subject, *Love and Respect: The Love She Most Desires; The Respect He Desperately Needs* by Emerson Eggerichs. I encourage every couple to read and discuss this book. The concepts it contains will impact their marriage relationship in a positive way.

As an example, a friend came to me seeking advice. When Fred first spoke with me, he indicated he was aware of the biblical admonition for men to love their wives as Christ loved the church, However, he pointed out this same passage of Scripture called for wives to respect their husbands. "And," he said, "she is not respectful of me." I suggested that though we might know the right thing to do, we are often reluctant to take the first step and fail to consider the other person may also be waiting for us to take the first step.

There is a great film called *Fireproof*, which I highly recommend. In it we get a glimpse of how difficult it can be (even when we do all the right things) to bring about reconciliation when a couple is estranged. It is important to remember reconciliation always starts with me; yet often there is an expectation the other person should go first. Perhaps the best lesson we might learn from this film is that love and respect

27

must be unconditional. We need not—indeed should not—wait for our spouse to make the first move.

Someone once related to me that his wife had a serious disagreement with her mother. His wife would not even call her father for fear her mother would pick up the phone. When over a year passed and there was no reconciliation in sight, my friend became concerned his wife's father, whose health was failing, might pass away. Although the father had played no part in the original argument, he was nonetheless suffering the consequences of the dispute between his wife and daughter. My friend was wise enough to recognize that if his father-in-law died, his wife would regret not having spoken to her father in more than a year. When he suggested she call her father, she flatly rejected the idea, saying, "He has a phone; he can call me."

Recognizing pride was the issue, he waited until his wife was out and placed a call to his mother-in-law, saying, "Was Betty ever able to get in touch with you? I know she's been trying to reach you." When his wife returned from the store, he told her that her mother had been trying to get hold of her. The pride issue overcome, his wife called her mother, all was forgiven and forgotten, and his deception was never discovered. Both mother and daughter resumed a dialogue as if nothing had ever happened. Please understand, I am neither recommending deception nor promoting the concept that the ends justify the means. I use this only to illustrate the effects of pride on relationships.

The lesson we might take from this is that pride can be a major problem for relationships. This may be the reason Scripture says, "God opposes the proud, but gives grace to the humble" (James 4:6).

Marriage is a solemn commitment and should be entered into only after much thought and prayer. Both husband and wife must approach marriage with a determination that it is a life-long relationship—a commitment before God.

In a typical relationship, many couples marry, enter careers, and then proceed to grow apart. One spouse may continue to expand his education while the other becomes a homemaker, or both may explore separate career paths. Any variety of similar scenarios leads to separate lives. Usually at the end of the day, both parties are too tired or unwilling to replay their day for the other. Or, if one happens to respond to the typical query of "How was your day, dear?" the spouse who asked may not even actively listen to the other's response.

In the New Testament, Paul encourages those contemplating marriage to be "equally yoked." The biblical reference depicts two animals yoked together. Those who have ever done any farming or horse logging, know the task is much more difficult if using two animals of differing strength or willingness to work as a team. Consider two animals (say a pig and a cow) yoked together and trying to pull a hay wagon. The picture may be comical, but the results would be undesirable, unless you simply wanted to have a good laugh or photo opportunity. Or, from a secular perspective, you might consider the old Native American saying: "A bird and a fish should not marry, for where would they make their home?"

The Web site www.eharmony.com provides computer matchmaking by comparing couples across multiple levels of compatibility. This is just another way of helping to assure couples are equally yoked.

When couples are "in love," they may trivialize important issues. It's easy to say, "Oh, that won't be a problem," or "We can overcome that." The reality is usually quite different. Little problems before marriage can become large problems after marriage. If leaving the cap off of a tube of toothpaste causes anxiety, imagine trying to agree where your child will attend church—or even *if* he or she is going to attend church. In one instance, a couple had never actually discussed whether or not they wanted children. Since the husband was older and had a family by a previous marriage, he had no desire for more children, while his wife (a much younger woman) wanted to have her own family. This issue would have resulted in the termination of the marriage had not a counselor intervened.

A close pastor friend of mine related the story of two people in his community who wanted to be married by him in his church. The woman was a Christian. The man was not. The pastor shared with the woman the Scripture verse about being unequally yoked. Yet the woman insisted that marrying a nonbeliever did not bother her. The pastor refused to marry the couple, and the woman left the church. One year later, and already divorced, the woman returned to the church. Please do not misunderstand. I am not saying the marriage of a Christian to a non-Christian never works. However, it can become a major obstacle to a happy marriage.

What does it mean to be equally yoked? Some people might consider this matchmaking—an effort to make sure couples enjoy the same things, have similar interests, and have compatible personalities. Computer-matchmaking services usually make an attempt to see that the couples are matched to some degree spiritually as well.

From a Christian point of view, spiritual compatibility takes on a much richer meaning. Some might think of spiritual compatibility as a denominational guideline (meaning Catholic should marry Catholic, or Protestant should marry Protestant). Others make a broader application. For example, one Christian should marry another Christian. But many people often miss the essence of Christianity. What exactly is a Christian?

When counseling couples contemplating marriage, my first endeavor is always to find out if the couples are equally yoked. During my initial counseling session, I state that I will marry the couple if both are Christians, or I will marry them if both are nonbelievers. However, I will not marry the couple if one is a believer and the other is not.

I explain I will give both individuals an opportunity at the conclusion of our counseling session to make a decision for Christ, based on the appropriate Scriptures they will read and discuss during the course of the counseling. I emphasize this kind of decision is an individual one made with all one's heart and mind. It is not to be taken lightly, and I do not want either individual to make a decision based on pleasing me or someone else. A decision to become a Christian must be carefully and intelligently considered. The decisions they make will affect the type and content of the wedding service I perform for them.

Since I am an associate pastor, I am the one often asked to marry couples from outside our church. Because our church is located in a scenic resort community, we receive many such requests. Since this is my opportunity to meet and get to know these couples, I first ask about their spiritual backgrounds. I often hear something like this: "My fiancé is Methodist and I'm Lutheran. But neither of us attends church very regularly."

During our first counseling session, I ask the couple this simple question to establish the essence of whether or not they are Christians: "If you died today and God said, 'Why should I let you into heaven?' how would you answer that question?" Most couples' response includes something like, "I'm a good person," or "I try to do the right things," or "I go to church regularly." I've even received similar answers from children of clergy. The bottom line is that many young people today, even those who have attended church for years, have no idea what it really means to be a Christian or, for that matter, what it takes to enter heaven. I believe this to be one of the reasons the divorce rate within the church is essentially the same as for couples outside the church. Churches today are often filled with many "nominal" Christians (i.e. Christians in name only).

Scripture records, "The disciples were called Christians first at Antioch" (Acts 11:26b). As defined in *Vine's Expository Dictionary of Biblical Words*, a disciple is "one who follows the teachings of Christ" and "one who believed upon Christ and confessed him."

John 3:16, perhaps the best-known verse in Scripture, says: "For God so loved the world that he gave his one and only Son, that whoever *believes* in him shall not perish but have eternal life" (bold Italics added for emphasis). This call to "believe" is repeated in Romans 10:9, where a clear explanation to the conditions for salvation is given by the Apostle Paul: "That if you confess with your mouth, 'Jesus is Lord,' and believe in your heart that God raised him from the dead, you will be saved." A further understanding of this calling can be found in Ephesians 2:8–10, "For it is by grace you have been saved, through faith—and this not of yourselves, it is the gift of God—not by works, so that no man can boast. For we are God's workmanship, created in Christ Jesus to do good works, which God prepared in advance for us to do."

The essential element for salvation is confessed belief in a risen Christ as Lord and Savior.

Our human nature suggests that, perhaps, this is too easy. We are tempted to feel we ought to play some larger role in our own salvation. Our problem, then, is as old as the ages. It began in the Garden of Eden when Satan tempted Eve. Satan has worked since then to corrupt the church and the minds of believers. He worked in the same way during Old Testament times to corrupt the Israelites. Satan uses the "traditions of man" to corrupt. For example, the *Talmud* (sixty books that contain the Jewish canonical laws) was passed down through tradition and contains detailed explanations of the commandments given to Moses on Mount Sinai. For example, one commandment of the Decalogue (in Exodus 20:9–10), "Six days you shall labor, … but the seventh day is the Sabbath of the LORD …" took Talmudic doctors four hundred sixteen sections to explain. Each section contains from eight to twenty divisions, giving the most minute directions for the observance of the Talmudic Sabbath laws. Tradition causes us to add to the Word of God in a pious attempt to "make God more understandable." Yet many Jews believe the Talmud to be as holy and binding as the Ten Commandments.

When questioned by the Pharisees about healing on the Sabbath, Jesus immediately referred to their tradition when he asked, "If any of you has a sheep and it falls into a pit on the Sabbath, will you not take hold of it and lift it out? How much more valuable is a man than a sheep! Therefore it is lawful to do good on the Sabbath" (Matthew 12:11–12). Jesus also cautioned, "For I tell you that unless your righteousness surpasses that of the Pharisees and the teachers of the law, you will certainly not enter the kingdom of heaven" (Matthew 5:20).

Today we find the church divided by tradition. We have made the same mistakes the Israelites made in the past. We have allowed traditions to separate us from God and other Christians, rather than to unite us and draw us closer to God. Christian traditions of baptism (immerse vs. sprinkle) and Communion (one cup or separate cups), among others, have served to divide Christians so that today we have numerous denominations—not united in Christ, but divided by tradition. It is my personal belief that what Satan has used to divide God's church God has used to grow His church.

In the following charts I have illustrated two marriages. In the first (Chart # 2), the couple is married and then the distractions of life cause them to gradually grow apart. In the next (Chart # 3), the two are married, grow in Christlikeness, and are drawn inexorably closer together as each becomes more like Christ. This second example is the goal toward which couples seeking a more intimate relationship strive.

Am I saying that only Christian marriages can succeed? That would be far from the truth. For one thing, this model only works for those who purposefully follow it. And statistically, Christians have as many failed marriages as do non-Christians. (However, it is only fair to point out these statistics include failed marriages like my own first marriage, which occurred before I became a Christian). I would suppose this is also true for the same reason that churches today are filled with people who never open their Bibles, never study Scripture, and never strive to become more like Christ.

It is this phenomenon that keeps many people from becoming Christians today. These individuals use the easy excuse: churches are filled with hypocrites. The reality is that nominal Christians often attend churches. These individuals claim the name of Christ, but do not truly know Him. That is why James recorded these words in the New Testament, "Show me your faith without deeds, and I'll show you my faith by what I do" (James 2:18b). Not a "works" theology, but rather, as James implies, faith in action.

33

Consider some of the ways the factors listed in this chart might work to distance a relationship. As couples move from single life to married life, each brings a separate group of friends to a relationship. These friendships do not always make the transition from "my friends" to "our friends." In addition, a husband may form new friendships through work, and a wife might find friends through neighborhood life or a separate career that, likewise, may not transition to be friends of both. One spouse may go on to advance his or her education, and one work to pay for that education. A husband may enjoy golf, and the wife horseback riding. Or, in another scenario, one may be career-oriented and the other stay home with the children. Both scenarios represent divergent points of focus.

It is important to recognize the potential for our work, our friendships, our differing interests, and even our differing levels of education to cause couples to grow apart.

CHART 2

Personal Growth Can Sometimes Lead to Separation

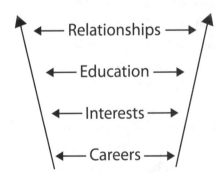

Notice in the chart 3 that as both husband and wife grow through the process of what Christians know as "sanctification" or growing to be more like Christ, they are inevitably drawn closer to each other. It should be noted also that God's plans for marriage can best be realized by couples who honor God and live in accordance with His plan.

34

CHART 3

Growth in Christ-likeness
Draws Couples Close Together

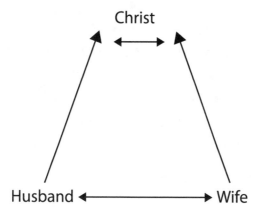

I don't believe it's possible to tell someone too many times that you love him/her. In addition, live out the expression, "Actions speak louder than words." Husbands, don't just tell your wife you love her, demonstrate your love with actions. Do the dishes, bring her flowers, remember your anniversary. Wives, don't just tell your husbands you respect them, demonstrate respect with your actions as well as with your words. Build him up, compliment him on good decisions, tell him about those things for which you respect him and why.

Lastly, I exhort all to read 1 Corinthians 13. This chapter contain some of the greatest words ever penned on what love is and what love is not. This list of how and how not to love is one my wife and I read and re-read. It offers a wonderful checklist of ways to improve our relationship. For example, love "keeps no record of wrongs" (verse 5) is sometimes a much-needed reminder we may be keeping a "file" on someone—some awful things done to us in the past we can use against them at a future date. This is not only a bad idea—it's not biblical either.

What might we take from this chapter on love that we can apply to help us beat the marriage odds? I believe there are two principles here.

35

> ### PRINCIPLE:
> The greater our will or determination for a successful marriage, the greater our odds are for the reality of a successful marriage.
>
> ### PRINCIPLE:
> Being equally yoked, or compatible, greatly increases the odds for a successful marriage.

BIBLICAL COMMENTARY ON LOVE

Proverbs 10:12 "Hatred stirs up dissension, but love covers over all wrongs."

This verse is a reminder of the effects of our actions—both positive and negative.

John 3:16 "For God so loved the world that he gave his one and only Son, that whoever believes in him shall not perish but have eternal life."

Perhaps the best-known verse in Scripture, this verse shows the true agape or unconditional love of God.

John 15:17 "This is my command: Love each other."

Jesus stated this, not as an option, but rather as a command. If God wants us to love even our enemies, how much more then should we love our spouse?

Romans 10: 9 "That if you confess with your mouth, 'Jesus is Lord' and believe in your heart that God raised him from the dead, you will be saved."

The essential element required if we are to call ourselves "Christians" is a confessed belief in a risen Christ as Lord and Savior.

Ephesians 2: 8–10 "For it is by grace you have been saved, through faith —and this not from yourselves, it is the gift of God—not by works, so that no man can boast. For we are God's workmanship, created in Christ Jesus to do good works, which God prepared in advance for us to do."

Grace is unmerited favor. We can't earn it and we don't deserve it. God knew that if we could find a way, our pride would cause us to take credit for something totally unearned and unmerited.

1 John 4:7–12 "Dear friends, let us love one another, for love comes from God. Everyone who loves has been born of God and knows God. Whoever does not love does not know God, because God is love. This is how God showed his love among us: He sent his one and only Son into the world that we might live through Him. This is love: Not that we loved God, but that he loved us and sent his Son as an atoning sacrifice for our sins. Dear friends, since God so loved us, we also ought to love one another. No one has ever seen God; but if we love one another, God lives in us and his love is made complete in us."

First John 4:20 plainly says we are liars if we claim to love God and do not love one another. John says this is not possible.

1 Corinthians 13:1–13 "If I speak in the tongues of men and of angels, but have not love, I am only a resounding gong or a clanging cymbal. If I have the gift of prophecy and can fathom all mysteries and all knowledge, and if I have a faith that can move mountains, but have not love, I am nothing. If I give all I possess to the poor and surrender my body to the flames, but have not love, I gain nothing.

"Love is patient, love is kind. It does not envy, it does not boast, it is not proud. It is not rude, it is not self-seeking, it is not easily angered, it keeps no record of wrongs. Love does not delight in evil but rejoices with the truth. It always protects, always trusts, always hopes, always perseveres.

"Love never fails. But where there are prophecies, they will cease; where there are tongues, they will be stilled; where there is knowledge, it will pass away. For we know in part and we prophesy in part, but when perfection comes, the imperfect disappears. When I was a child,

I thought like a child, I reasoned like a child. When I became a man, I put childish ways behind me. Now we see but a poor reflection as in a mirror; then we shall see face to face. Now I know in part; then I shall know fully, even as I am fully known.

And now these three remain: faith, hope and love. But the greatest of these is love."

My wife and I use the list presented in these verses as a "how to" and "how not to" list—a way to help us evaluate our own love. For instance, are we keeping track of wrongs done to us, are we being rude to one another, are we being easily angered, etc.? In other words, it can serve as an effective checklist.

2 Corinthians 6:14–16 "Do not be yoked together with unbelievers. For what do righteousness and wickedness have in common? Or what fellowship can light have with darkness? What harmony is there between Christ and Belial? What does a believer have in common with an unbeliever? What agreement is there between the temple of God and idols? For we are the temple of the living God."

Have you ever asked yourself why God forbade the Israelites to intermarry with pagans? If you read closely the Old Testament, you will see whenever the Israelites broke this restriction it always ended badly for them. They departed from their faith; they began to worship false idols and to build altars in high places. God's desire is for His people to be holy and set apart—not because He wants us to be elitist snobs, but because He wants us to be "in the world, and not of it."

Ephesians 5:33 "However, each one of you also must love his wife as he loves himself, and the wife must respect the husband."

This is a key command. Women most often feel unloved, while men most often feel disrespected. Troubles in a marriage often begin when one of these two conditions is not being met.

SALVATION VERSES

Here are four spiritual laws for consideration:

• First, God Loves you and has a wonderful plan for your life.

John 3:16 "For God so loved the world that he gave his one and only Son, that whoever believes in Him shall not perish but have eternal live."

Romans 5:8 "God demonstrates his own love for us in: While we were still sinners, Christ died for us."

Jeremiah 29:11 "'For I know the plans I have for you,' declares the LORD. 'Plans to prosper you and not to harm you, plans to give you hope and a future.'"

• Second, we are separated from God by our own sinful nature.

Romans 3:23–24 "For all have sinned and fall short of the glory of God, and are justified freely by his grace through the redemption that came by Christ Jesus."

Romans 6:23 "For the wage of sin is death ..." (spiritual separation from God).

• Third, God has provided a way for us to be in union with him for eternity.

John 14:6 "... I am the way and the truth and the life. No one comes to the Father except through me."

Romans 10:9–10 "That if you confess with your mouth, 'Jesus is Lord,' and believe in your heart that God raised him from the dead, you will be saved. For it is with your heart that you believe and are justified, and it is with your mouth that you confess and are saved."

• And Fourth, God has left it to us to take the final step. We must accept the free gift of unmerited favor He has offered.

Revelation 3:20 "Here I am! I stand at the door and knock. if anyone hears my voice and opens the door, I will come in ..."

John 1:12 "Yet to all who received him, to those who believe in his name, he gave the right to become children of God."

Remember, we are not called to blind faith, but rather to a faith in a risen Christ. His resurrection was witnessed not only by His disciples, but by over 500 others as well.

1 Corinthians 15:3–6 "… Christ died for our sins … he was buried … he was raised on the third day according to the Scriptures … he appeared to Peter, and then to the Twelve. After that, he appeared to more than five hundred …"

Ephesians 2: 8–10 "For it is by grace you have been saved, through faith—and this not from yourselves, it is the gift of God—not by works, so that no one can boast. For we are God's workmanship, created in Christ Jesus to do good works, which God prepared in advance for us to do."

Chapter V

TRUST

THE FOUNDATION FOR A LASTING RELATIONSHIP

Like any physical structure, a marriage must be built on a solid foundation. Honesty is, of course, a key ingredient in the foundation of any marriage. Along with honesty must follow trust. The reason this is so important is simply that marriage partners, like close personal friends, will often tell us things we don't necessarily want to hear. When this occurs, if we do not trust the other person's judgment we will simply reject the criticism as unjust or untrue. Yet when we have confidence in our critics, we are able to appreciate the gift of seeing ourselves as others see us.

My wife, because she knows me so well, often gives me a look into myself in a way that not many could. For example, when I was commenting on the behavior of one of my children one day, she said, "Well, he comes by it honestly." By this she meant that I also am guilty of the behavior I was criticizing. I immediately asked, "You mean I do that?" It is very important when someone tells us something we might not like to hear about ourselves that we thoughtfully consider the comment, for often these are opportunities to get a better and more objective look at ourselves. It is to our advantage to train ourselves to view criticism as an opportunity for personal growth.

The trust required for a lasting and sound relationship is thus built on honesty. A byproduct of this trust is openness. For it is only in a relationship based on honesty and trust that we can allow ourselves to become open and vulnerable. Building relationships that will last is a process, which is developed over time, and is based on solid and proven elements of character. Mike Huckabee has written a wonderful book on this subject, entitled *Character Makes a Difference: Where I'm From, Where I've Been, and What I Believe.* Many people today, on both sides of the political spectrum, no longer trust politicians to look out for their best interests. And, while we may not trust our politicians, it is essential we trust the person we choose to spend the rest of our life with.

Many of the issues in *Beating the Marriage Odds* are interrelated. For instance, good communication (Chapter VI) also requires honesty, openness and trust—all of which are essential in a healthy marriage. Together these three core values underlie almost every aspect of the marriage relationship.

As an example of just how important this issue of trust can be, let's look at a situation taken from real life: Bob's father had died of lung cancer and his mother suffered from emphysema, both smoking-related illnesses. His fiancée, Betty, had recently begun smoking. Although Bob thought he loved Betty, he insisted he would not marry a smoker. Thus, as a result of his declaration, Betty told Bob she would quit smoking; yet for the entire period of their engagement she continued to smoke behind his back. Try to imagine his response when, on their wedding day, he kissed her at the altar and found out she had been smoking. Then, in the limousine ride from the church to their reception, she revealed she had never really given up smoking and, further, had no intention of doing so. And, though they struggled through this obstacle, the lack of trust continued to be an issue for them for many years. Through counseling, Bob and Betty eventually came to recognize this foundational issue had initiated many of their relational problems.

The issue of trust is one of the reasons Jesus said the only grounds for divorce was marital infidelity or adultery. Once someone violates trust in a marriage (and there can be no greater violation of trust than infidelity), it can take years to rebuild that trust. It is a Herculean task to rebuild broken trust.

Although adultery can be used as biblical grounds for divorce, it need not result in divorce. I have counseled a number of couples through these treacherous waters. If one or both parties wish to save the marriage relationship after such a violation of trust, it is possible. It can be, and usually is, a difficult and painful process. However, restoring the marriage honors God, as evidenced in the Scriptures, where it is recorded God hates divorce (see Malachi 2:16).

Marriages that successfully negotiate these painful trials usually emerge as among the strongest and healthiest of marital relationships. You have heard the cliché that time heals all wounds. Once trust has been destroyed in a relationship, however, the time required to restore that trust can become a difficult, and sometimes insurmountable, obstacle. The mistrust introduced into a relationship by the sin of adultery is one of the direct consequences of that sin.

Sin always, and I repeat, always has consequences. In Scripture we see the case of David's adulterous affair with Bathsheba. This sin cost David the life of their first child. This story can be found in 2 Samuel 12:9–14. Here we see the prophet Nathan sent by the Lord to rebuke David for his sin:

> "'Why did you despise the word of the LORD by doing what is evil in his eyes? You struck down Uriah the Hittite with the sword and took his wife to be your own. You killed him with the sword of the Ammonites. Now, therefore, the sword will never depart from your house, because you despised me and took the wife of Uriah the Hittite to be your own.'
>
> "This is what the LORD says: "Out of your own household I am going to bring calamity upon you.

Before your very eyes I will take your wives and give them to one who is close to you, and he will lie with your wives in broad daylight. You did it in secret, but I will do this thing in broad daylight before all Israel.'"

Then David said to Nathan, "I have sinned against the LORD."

Nathan replied, "The LORD has taken away your sin. You are not going to die. But because by doing this you have made enemies of the Lord show utter contempt, *the son born to you will die.*"

Not recognizing the consequences of his own actions, one of the young men I counseled following an adulterous relationship complained to me, "My wife calls me ten times a day. She wants to know where I am and whom I'm with. She's always checking up on me." I reminded him it was he who had violated the trust he had once enjoyed, and his wife's constant questioning was the price he now paid for violating that trust. With time and hard work, trust can be rebuilt. It requires the violated partner be willing to forgive and the offending partner be willing to patiently work at rebuilding that trust.

Forgiving and forgetting are two separate things. Forgiving, which is required for healing, is not the same as forgetting. We may never forget, but if we truly forgive others we will no longer use the instance as a weapon against them. In his book, *70 x 7 and Beyond: Mystery of the Second Chance*, Monty Christensen (someone who truly knows the meaning of forgiveness) points out Scripture records in Isaiah 43:25 that God says, "I, even I, am he who blots out your transgressions, for my own sake, and remembers your sins no more," but we humans do remember. Yet to truly live the happy and victorious life, we are called to use our experiences of hurts and trials to help others. Paul explained this in II Corinthians 1:4, "… so that we can comfort those in any trouble with the comfort we ourselves have received from God."

Understand that "… suffering produces perseverance; perseverance, character; and character, hope" (Romans 5:3–4). The process of healing takes time, but this process can be speeded up considerably by refocusing our attentions to the hurts and needs of others. Self-pity is not a helpful healing agent.

A key thought to remember is: There is no guarantee a violated trust can be regained. It is solely dependent on another individual. Consider the risk you take in violating the trust another has placed in you. Such a violation could and, in fact, usually does cause an undesirable outcome (one you may be helpless to change).

When counseling couples contemplating marriage, I often say, "I don't trust my wife." Invariably, I get a shocked reaction to this pronouncement. I then go on to explain that my wife, like myself, is human, and therefore unworthy of trust. However, I do trust "Christ in her," a seemingly small, yet significant difference. The reality is both my wife and I have a sinful nature. John 15:5 record the words of Jesus, "… apart from me you can do nothing." All people—and this certainly includes Christians—have the capacity to let us down and to disappoint us. God, on the other hand, is completely trustworthy! The idea being that God, who instituted marriage, is the only One who can and will empower us in our marriages if we ask Him.

Jealousy, a very destructive force, is also an issue of trust since it has, at its root, mistrust. I have seen marriages torn apart by completely unfounded jealousy. Often this tendency toward mistrust can be spotted early in a relationship. It must be addressed because left unchecked and to its own natural course, jealousy will destroy even the best of relationships.

There can be many reasons for mistrust. A person may have been hurt in a previous relationship or in a family situation. Adult children of alcoholics are often mistrustful. They also frequently have a problem telling the truth, as a result of carrying a family secret that needed to be kept from the outside world. This is one reason why it is important to complete and evaluate a family history before entering into marriage.

Many times I hear couples say, "I'm marrying him (or her) not his (or her) family." Yet consistently we find issues of physical, emotional, or substance abuse, which are passed on from generation to generation. These matters are best addressed early on, rather than when a crisis occurs quite unexpectedly down the road. We'll take a closer look at family histories and the impact they might have on a marriage in Chapter XI, "In-laws/Out-laws."

In Chapter VII, "Finances," we talk about the need for couples to set boundaries and agree on spending limits. For example, a couple might decide that any expenditure over $100 must be agreed upon by the two of them before such a purchase is made. And though the amount may vary, the important thing is that both parties agree to the arrangement. Thus, any violation of this agreement also would become a violation of trust.

Likewise, telling an embarrassing story about a spouse in public, which was learned in confidence, can violate a trust. Here again, communication plays an important role. Talking about such things first, before airing them in public can avoid many confrontations. Or even asking, "Would it embarrass you if I told them the story of …?" could prevent a serious argument.

What important principle might we draw from this chapter?

PRINCIPLE:
In a marriage, your word is quite literally your bond.
To destroy that bond is to undermine the very foundation
of the marriage!

BIBLICAL COMMENTARY ON A SOLID FOUNDATION

Exodus 20:5 "… I, the LORD your God, am a jealous God, punishing the children for the sin of the fathers to the third and fourth generation of those who hate me."

When we talk about "sins of the fathers," we refer to generational sins, some of which might arguably be considered genetic. (Children of alcoholics are at greater risk of becoming alcoholics—some argue this is genetic, but, in either case, the risk should be acknowledged.) Still other sins are simply passed on to our siblings as they observe our behavior. (Spousal or child abuse would fall into this category.)

Psalm 118:8 "It is better to take refuge in the LORD than to trust in man."

Many times in my life I have been let down by those I trusted, yet never has the Lord broken a biblical promise to me. We should be careful not to set ourselves up for disappointment. Recognize that even those closest to us can, and often do, disappoint us.

Proverbs 3:5–6 "Trust in the LORD with all your heart and lean not on your own understanding; in all your ways acknowledge him, and he will make your paths straight."

We must acknowledge our own fallibility and place our trust where it will not disappoint us. Not only can others disappoint us, our own understandings can disappoint us. Many times I have argued with my wife about a point on which I felt sure, only to find out later I was mistaken.

Proverbs 12:22 "The LORD detests lying lips, but he delights in men who are truthful."

Not surprisingly, truth pleases the Lord, while dishonesty offends Him.

John 14:1 "Do not let your hearts be troubled. Trust in God; trust also in me."

Trust in God and in Jesus Christ never disappoints us. It is God's desire that we trust in Him.

1 Corinthians 4:2 "Now it is required that those who have been given a trust must prove faithful."

Trust must be earned, and once lost is very difficult to reestablish.

Leviticus 19:11 "Do not steal. Do not lie. Do not deceive one another."

God's commandments given to Moses at Mount Sinai include important moral issues, such as lying, stealing, deception, swearing falsely, and adultery.

Proverbs 19:22 "What a man desires is unfailing love; better to be poor than a liar."

God favors a poor, truthful person over a rich liar.

Colossians 3:5–10 "Put to death, therefore, whatever belongs to your earthly nature: sexual immorality, impurity, lust, evil desires and greed, which is idolatry. Because of these the wrath of God is coming. You used to walk in these ways, in the life you once lived. But now you must rid yourselves of all such things as these: anger, rage, malice, slander, and filthy language from your lips. Do not lie to each other, since you have taken off your old self with its practices and have put on the new self, which is being renewed in knowledge in the image of its Creator."

These verses are a wonderful reminder that God, through the redemption, has made us into new beings. As Christians we are no longer slaves to sin and the old self; we are new creations.

1 John 1:10 "If we claim we have not sinned, we make him out to be a liar and his word has no place in our lives."

This verse should serve to remind us all of our capacity for self-deception.

Exodus 20:14 "You shall not commit adultery."

The commandment here against adultery made God's "Top Ten" list.

1 Samuel 11 records David's sin with Bathsheba and his consequent sin, which caused the death of her husband. In 1 Samuel 12 we see God's judgment on David for those sins. In verses 11 and 13–14 the prophet Nathan says: "This is what the LORD says: 'Out of your own household I am going to bring calamity upon you.' "… The LORD has taken away your sin. You are not going to die. But because by doing this you have made the enemies of the LORD show utter contempt, the son born to you will die."

David was forgiven because he admitted his sin before God, but there were still consequences. Since David had compounded the sin of adultery by then having Bathsheba's husband killed, the consequences were severe indeed.

I try never to forget sin always has consequences. Sometimes, as in David's case, they are not immediate. But we should never deceive ourselves by thinking we are getting away with anything. God cannot be deceived.

John 15:5 "… apart from me you can do nothing."

Jesus reminds us that left to our own devices we are inclined by our own human nature to sin.

Chapter VI

COMMUNICATION
The Leading Cause of Marital Breakdowns

Communication problems are one of the single greatest causes of failed relationships. Psychologist Larry Crabb discusses this in his book *The Marriage Builder: A Blueprint for Couples and Counselors*. He notes that communication problems inevitably result when people pursue self-centered goals, but sometimes problems also arise because individuals have not learned how to communicate clearly and efficiently. Communication involves the sending and receiving of messages. Messages may be either verbal (with words) or nonverbal (with gestures, tone of voice, facial expressions, written on paper, images on a computer screen, actions, gifts, or even silence). Communication is a *learned* interaction. When it is faulty, it can, and should be, improved.

Relationships in crisis can often be reduced to a formula that would look something like this: $S + L + P = C$. In this formula, S would represent stress, L would represent a lack of coping skills, and P would represent perspective. One or all of these lead to C, the crisis. The counselor's task in helping couples to deal with a crisis, then becomes the reduction of stress, the teaching of new coping skills, and/or the offering of a new perspective.

Communication breakdowns or inefficiencies almost always result in increased tensions within a relationship. One of the main reasons for such breakdowns is because most of us have never learned some of the basic skills required to communicate effectively. This chapter is intended to assist with those skills. In some cases, the skills may already be familiar; in others they will be new concepts. Since we are all creatures of habit, and habits are formed over time, it will take time and practice to implement these new skills. Be patient and work at these skills.

Communication problems play a central role in interpersonal relationships. Therefore, this chapter will perhaps be the most important chapter for many of us, one well worth reading, implementing, rereading, and practicing. Remember, old habits simply cannot be replaced overnight.

Just as in the military, there are what I call "rules of engagement" in relationships. I first read about these simple rules in the book *Christian Counseling* by Dr. Gary Collins, which had been reprinted from Sven Wahlroos' book *Family Communication*. These basic rules have changed little over the years. Studying this list can help us recognize any bad communication habits we employ. We must resist the temptation to point to our spouse's bad habits. These principles are for personal application. Remember, we cannot change another person; we can change only ourselves.

RULES OF ENGAGEMENT

1. Actions speak louder than words. Often we send mixed messages when our nonverbal message is contrary to our verbal message.

For example: Shirley tells her husband, John, she has no objection to his going golfing, yet the disgusted look on her face clearly indicates she is not pleased with the idea. If John goes, and has not paid attention, he will be quite disturbed when she later tells him all the things he should have done rather than go golfing. "But you told me I could go!" will likely be his response. Often mixed messages can lead to inappropriate responses, further complicating the communication.

2.   Define what is important and stress it. Define what is unimportant and deemphasize it or ignore it.

As an example: John was retelling a story at a family gathering. His wife interrupted the story to insist it happened on a Friday not a Saturday, and an argument ensued. Whether the event happened on a Friday at 10 AM or on Saturday at 2 PM is of little consequence, yet such trivial details frequently result in arguments. Note: This is very similar to pointless faultfinding, which is discussed later in this chapter.

3.   Communicate in ways that show respect for the other person's worth as a human being. Avoid beginning statements with absolutes, such as "You never ..."

For example: Tom says to his wife, "You never have dinner ready on time. I work hard all day, while you lie around the house and watch soap operas. I can't even come home to a decent meal."

Note that Tom has made a number of assumptions here: 1) His wife *never* has dinner ready when he comes home (assumes she has never once had his dinner ready when he came home); 2) His wife sits around *all day* watching soap operas (assumes he knows what she is doing each moment of every day); and 3) He can't come home to a *decent* meal (assumes she is incapable of, or refuses to, prepare a decent meal). In addition, his "you never" comment is a sweeping generalization, as illustrated in the next point, and thus to be avoided.

4.   Be clear and specific in your communication. Avoid vagueness.

For example: Saying, "I may play golf with the guys sometime this week" (vague), versus "The guys want to play golf this afternoon. If I play I won't be home in time for dinner. I could grab a bite at the club. Would that be okay, or is there any reason that won't work?"

5.   Be realistic and reasonable in your statements. Avoid exaggeration and sentences that begin with, "You always ..."

For example, "You always insist on having your way. I never get to have a say in anything." Note: While we might think such sweeping statements are true at the time, closer examination rarely bears this out.

6. Test all your assumptions verbally by asking if they are accurate. Avoid acting until this is done. (See Chapter IX, "Mind Games.")

As an example, instead of the statement in the example above, you might say: "I feel like you are the one making all the decisions and I don't have a voice in our affairs. Can you give me some examples of when I've made the choices or you asked for my input?"

7. Recognize that each event can be seen from various points of view. Do not assume others see everything just as you do or they should see them exactly as you do.

For example: Tom comes home and announces, "I bought a new car today. We needed it, with gas prices going up every day. You'll love it. It's purple, my favorite color."

Note: First, Tom has failed to recognize his wife was perfectly content with the old car. Second, they had no car payments, and any savings in gas will be eaten up by the new car payments. Third, his wife hates purple. While it might be all right to buy a purple T-shirt for himself without consulting his wife, a major purchase such as an automobile is another matter. In Chapter V on Trust and in Chapter VII on Finances, we discuss the importance of shared decision-making about major purchases and within agreed-upon spending limits.

8. Recognize that your close friends and family members are experts on you and your behavior. Avoid the tendency to deny their observations about you.

For example: Shirley tells her husband he has a tendency not to hear people when they speak to him. Tom argues that he hears just fine. His best friend laughs and confirms what Shirley has said. Tom jokingly says he hears all he wants to hear, but he dismisses their concerns completely. Tom may need to have his hearing checked. Or it's also possible

Tom's physical hearing is fine, but his emotional hearing is impaired. That is, he hears only what he wants to hear.

9. Recognize that disagreement can be a meaningful form of communication. Avoid destructive arguments. (See Chapter VIII, "Fighting Fair—The Upside of Arguments.")

This is a most import point to remember. Consider the following example: Tom and Shirley can't agree on a new car. He wants a red pickup truck for use on his hunting trips. She wants a white sport utility vehicle to haul all of the kids and their sports equipment. They can't afford both. They agree to disagree for the moment and postpone the decision until they can both reach agreement. After several weeks, Tom sees a new combination vehicle that gets better gas mileage than a truck yet has a small truck bed and four doors. He tells Shirley, and she agrees it is the perfect compromise. They ask a trusted friend to pick the color—red or white. They both are happy with the choices they've made together.

10. Be honest and open about your feelings and viewpoints. Bring up all significant points, even if you are afraid doing so will disturb another person. Speak the truth in love. Avoid sullen silence.

For example: Tom tells Shirley the purchase of a new barbecue for the backyard is ill advised at this time since he has just lost his job. Shirley goes into a tirade and silences Tom with her outburst. The result is that no meaningful discussion has taken place. Tom is frustrated and Shirley is frustrated, yet there has been no resolution to the issue at hand. Tom has not shared his fears about an uncertain future, nor his feeling that Shirley is being reckless with their family spending at a time when he is worried about putting food on the table. Shirley has not shared anything but anger at being denied a want. Any meaningful discussion of wants versus needs has not taken place.

11. Do not put down and/or manipulate the other person with tactics such as ridicule, interrupting, name calling, changing the subject, bullying, blaming, bugging, sarcasm, criticism, pouting,

inducing guilt, etc. Avoid the one-upmanship game—it is simply a controlling behavior.

For example: Ken says he has given up trying to talk with Susan. Anything controversial always ends with Susan screaming at him. As a result, he simply stuffs his feelings. Susan has found her outbursts end all discussions so she uses them to control and avoid unpleasant situations. This type of behavior left unchecked could eventually destroy their relationship. One day Ken may simply have had enough and walk out. Susan would thus be left to wonder what happened, not recognizing the role she herself played in this repeated drama.

12. Be more concerned about how your communication affects others than about what you intended. Avoid becoming bitter if you are misunderstood. Miscommunication results in misunderstandings. Always strive for clarity. If you sense you have been misunderstood, restate your communication using different words.

For example: Bob thinks their house is badly in need of repainting. The paint is peeling, and he hates the color. What he says to his wife is, "I hate our house. We need to change it." Dorothy instantly becomes defensive: "I love our house, and we're not going to change a thing." Bob should have recognized his error and attempted to clarify what he was saying. A clearer message could have been sent had he said, "The paint is beginning to peel and look bad; as long as we need to repaint, I've never particularly liked this color. Do you have any suggestions for a new color—something we both might like?"

13. Accept all feelings and try to understand why others feel and act as they do. Understand feelings cannot be denied, and avoid the tendency to say, "You shouldn't feel like that."

For example: Dorothy says to Bob, "You did a lousy job of cleaning the driveway. You left piles of leaves everywhere, and you didn't put away the broom when you finished."

Bob replies, "I feel like I'm being scolded by my mother when you talk like that."

"Don't be silly," Dorothy says. "Just do it right the first time and I won't have to say anything."

Dorothy, without realizing it, has just denied Bob's feelings. And, in fact, she has added to his feelings of inadequacy with her additional statement. A better response might have been, "I'm sorry, I didn't mean to be overly critical or to seem unappreciative. It probably would have been better if I had simply said, 'Thanks, and when you have time could you please put the leaves in a bag?'"

14. Be tactful, considerate, and courteous. Avoid taking advantage of the other person's feelings.

For example: Shirley arrives to take her friend to a luncheon and says, "Is that what you intend to wear to the luncheon?" Perhaps a more diplomatic comment might have been, "I spoke with Marilyn and she informed me that most of the women are getting dressed up for the luncheon. I'm sorry I was late, but I had to change into something a little dressier."

Note: This point is similar to #18. Humor that is appropriate for a very close friend may offend another. Be sensitive to the person you are addressing.

15. Ask appropriate questions and listen carefully. Avoid preaching or lecturing.

For instance, asking questions helps assure that the other person has an opportunity to contribute to the conversation. People are generally more attracted to a person who lets them do most of the talking. Asking questions flatters people and shows that you value their opinions. It also enhances listening skills, since it would be extremely rude to ask a question and then ignore the person's response.

16. Do not use excuses. Avoid falling for the excuses of others.

For example, Peter has been out of work for six months. He sits around the house and watches television while his wife waits tables at the local restaurant. Peter says, "There's no point in my looking for work; we're in a soft economy."

Here we have a situation that involves points # 10, # 9, and perhaps # 4 as well. A good friend should lovingly confront Peter, speaking clearly and honestly, not shying away from a difficult subject.

17. Speak kindly, politely, and softly. Avoid nagging, yelling, or whining.

As an example, Tom comes home out of sorts after a bad day at the office. In addition, he has an important meeting scheduled for later that night. He begins to loudly berate his wife, Shirley, for not having dinner ready. Tom continues his tirade until Shirley leaves the room in tears.

Often we take out our frustrations on those closest to us. We can become agitated at not being understood or frustrated that we have not won someone to our position. This can lead us to increase the volume of our speech.

Note: Increased volume seldom increases the comprehension level of the listener. In fact, it often causes them to shut down or cease listening, further locking their position. Perhaps you have witnessed an enraged customer become increasingly irate, while at the same time the store clerk becomes more entrenched in his position. Likewise, most of us have had opportunity to witness a voice of calm reason win the day.

18. Recognize the value of humor and seriousness. Avoid destructive teasing.

For instance, humor, when used appropriately, can ease tension and relieve a difficult situation. Used inappropriately, it can make a bad situation worse. Knowing when and where not to use humor requires knowledge of the person you are dealing with, as well as how he/she responds in different situations. As a general rule, if you are not sure of the person or his/her response in a given situation, avoid using humor. If you attempt humor and someone reacts badly, say simply, "I'm sorry; that was inappropriate. I was just trying to lighten the situation." Then return to a serious discussion of the issue, perhaps by saying something like, "How do you think we can best resolve this?"

Teasing a person who is already upset is like poking a stick at a tiger. You can expect a response, though it may not be the one you desire.

I would highly recommend everyone study these rules of engagement. Practice them. Discuss them with your spouse. And then agree to point out to each other when you note an inappropriate response. Learning to accept criticism is the first step to improved relationships! I cannot overemphasize this point.

The very title of the best-selling book by Dr. John Gray, *Men Are from Mars, Women Are from Venus: A Practical Guide for Improving Communication and Getting What You Want in Your Relationships,* gives a clue to the extent of the problem men and women experience with communication. I must admit at times it seems like my wife and I are speaking two entirely different languages.

The reasons for poor communication are manifold. In my own case, at times I do not hear (a result of an actual physical hearing loss). On still other occasions, I misunderstand what my wife is trying to communicate (a result of the language problem mentioned above—we use words differently). Occasionally, my wife or I have been known to think one thing and actually say another. Lastly, I must admit that, at times, I do not listen.

To illustrate this, let me use myself as an example. I am a very focused person (which is to say that multi-tasking and I are not well acquainted). I am one who cannot walk and chew gum at the same time. Often, when I'm working on my computer, my wife will ask me a question and I will respond with a simple "yes" or "no." Since my wife knows me so well, she usually follows up with another, more revealing question, "Do you have any idea what I just asked you?" (By now she's managed to get my attention.) The answer to this second question is usually, "No!" My wife's next question is always: "Then why did you answer me?" To which I reply, "Because I'm doing something else, and I didn't want to lose my train of thought." Since we have been through this scenario so many times, and because we have learned to accept each other's vagaries, we can laugh at these situations. She has learned that I am single-minded, and I have learned to tune in by the second question and listen to what she is saying.

The important thought here would be: take the time to learn how your partner communicates. If your spouse is a bad listener or hard of hearing, understand that extra effort will be required to communicate effectively.

Typically, women are better listeners than men. However, if you sense that listening is a problem for you, it is possible to train yourself to be a better listener. If you're not sure if you have a problem with listening, ask your spouse or a friend to tell you if they think you do not listen well. If you determine this to be a problem, you can test yourself by repeating what you think you heard. I highly recommend practicing this active listening technique. You'll be amazed at the results. It will not only help to develop your listening skills, it will also greatly increase your ability to communicate accurately and effectively.

This technique is a very important way to improve communication in a relationship. A counseling professor once referred to this technique as the "drive-through" technique. For example, we go to a drive-through restaurant and place the following order: "Two hamburgers, a Coke, one order of fries, and an orange drink." An unseen voice replies, "That was two burgers, an order of fries, a Coke, and an orange drink. Is that right?" In this manner, any miscommunication can be corrected and we may actually get what we ordered.

Another excellent example from a personal experience would be: Once, my wife and I were driving home from a counseling class at the university. We began disagreeing about something we had just studied. Our conversation became more animated as we loudly disagreed. I decided to apply the "drive-through" technique, which we had just learned that day in class. I told my wife, "This is what I just heard you say," and I proceeded to recount what I thought she had said. "No," she practically yelled, "that's not what I said at all." She then repeated what she had just said, using different words. "That's what I was saying," I protested. To which she replied, "Well, that's what I thought you were saying, so I couldn't understand why you were arguing with me."

This is truly an amazing technique and can be used to clear up a great many misunderstandings, whether hearing- or listening-related. I would highly recommend whenever you are experiencing problems communicating that you use the "drive-through" technique to assure you've really heard what was said!

Another useful communication method is the "speaker-listener" technique. The need for this approach often becomes apparent when, in the midst of a disagreement and in a rush to make our point, we over-talk the other person. (We do this by talking while the other person is still speaking, and often by a simultaneous raising of our voice.) An additional indicator of the need for the "speaker-listener" technique is when conversations begin to get loud and combative. This technique assures that both parties slow down, listen, and do not over-talk the other party. Slowing down the pace also serves to help keep tempers in check.

It works like this. One party, the speaker, holds an object (a pen, a ruler, or any object will do). Only the person holding the object is allowed to speak. The other party must wait his or her turn, until the speaker is through and passes the object to the listener, who now becomes the speaker and can respond.

The effect of this technique is to slow down a disagreement, prevent over-talking, and improve listening. It may be combined with the "drive-through" technique with excellent results. To illustrate, let's use the example of Tom and Ellen. Both Tom and Ellen are prone to interrupt each other. As a result, each would talk louder and louder in an attempt to make their points. The "speaker-listener" technique forced them to slow down and not over-talk their spouse. It helped in allowing each to stop and listen to what the other was saying and to keep the conversation from escalating into a shouting match.

It is not uncommon for couples in a hurry to make a point, or perhaps fearful of forgetting it, to over-talk one another. In some instances, this is simply due to poor listening habits. And, as we all know, habits are hard to break. This technique is an excellent way to help improve listening skills, since it forces each person to pay attention to what the other is saying. If you're afraid of forgetting something, simply take notes as the other person is speaking.

I would recommend the use of this "speaker-listener" technique whenever a discussion begins to spiral out of control or whenever the volume of a conversation starts increasing. If over-talking by either party is taking place, it's a good time to pull out the "talking stick."

Right now might be a good occasion to point out there are times in every relationship when the parties cannot agree. That's all right. Sometimes it is necessary to agree to disagree and revisit the issue at another time.

Allow me to use another personal example. My wife and I could not agree on fabric for a new sofa we were planning to purchase. I wanted a light plaid, while she wanted a dark print. Though it took nearly five years, we eventually agreed on a fabric we both loved. We bought neither a light plaid (which I now think would have been an awful choice) nor a dark print (which my wife now feels would have been equally as inappropriate).

The passage of time often brings a new and unseen alternative solution to a seemingly unsolvable impasse. For example, John's wife wanted to set up the family's TV room in what was currently serving as their recreation room. (This room, she reasoned, was much larger and more suitable, but it contained the husband's pride and joy—his pool table.) Neither John nor Kathy would give an inch. "The TV room is just too small to accommodate guests," Kathy protested. "I'm not giving up my pool table," replied John. And so it went for nearly a year.

Then, one day, a wise friend suggested an alternative neither had considered that would satisfy both needs—a larger TV room without disposing of John's cherished pool table. The couple moved the pool table into the office/library (large enough to accommodate such a sizeable piece of furniture) and then moved the office furniture to the former TV room. Kathy and John were both happy with the new arrangement. Time and a fresh viewpoint contributed to this resolution.

It is good to remember alternate solutions are not always evident in the midst of a disagreement. For that reason, it is wise to allow time for fresh thought or to seek another opinion. When seeking a fresh opinion, try to find an objective opinion from someone whose opinions both can respect. In other words, a wife saying, "My mother agrees with me" will probably not have the desired affect.

The key thought to remember here is: when at an impasse and agreement seems impossible, agree to disagree. Allow time for alternative solutions. Seek an outside opinion from an agreed-upon arbitrator. I would recommend this only if both agree to abide by that person's recommendations.

There are at least five levels of communication. The lowest levels of what I call the "communication pool" (see Chart 4 below) include clichés and platitudes (Level 1) and gossip (Level 2). These shallow communications consist of such things as hellos, good-byes, simple gossip, and repeating of facts. At the deepest end of the communication pool are feelings (Level 4) and intimacy (Level 5). Communication at this level deals with how we feel about issues, such as how we are affected by the actions or words of another person.

Note: We can choose to think or to do, but we cannot choose feelings. To deny someone's feelings is to deny reality. If someone is hurt or angry or confused, then we must explore the cause of those feelings to find the root of the problem. To fail to do so is to encourage unresolved conflict. This level (feelings) is where real growth occurs in relationships. It is most important couples learn to explore these deeper levels (feelings and intimacy) of the communication pool. These deep waters, however, are troubling and new to many of us. As a result, we must force ourselves into these depths. Getting comfortable in the deep end of the communication pool is essential to the healthy growth and development of a relationship. The midpoint in this imaginary swimming pool (Level 3) is called the opinion or idea level. And since conflicts arise out of differing opinions and ideas, this is the level at which arguments and disagreements rear their ugly heads.

It is common for couples to come to this mid-level in the communication pool, and, rather than deal with difficult issues by jumping into the deep end, simply retreat to the shallow end of the pool. Conflict is avoided; however, resolution is not achieved. Many couples follow this routine for years before one or both reach a level of frustration that leads them either to counseling or divorce.

CHART 4   **Communication Pool**

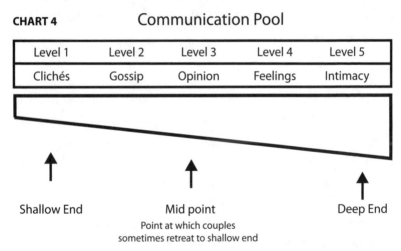

Level 1	Level 2	Level 3	Level 4	Level 5
Clichés	Gossip	Opinion	Feelings	Intimacy

Shallow End   Mid point   Deep End

Point at which couples
sometimes retreat to shallow end

Pastor Rick Warren, of Saddleback Church in Southern California, talks about a "tunnel of truth," referring to the need for honesty in communication. This is especially critical to achieve the intimacy level of communication when moving from what I call the "shallow end" (clichés) to the "deep end" (intimacy) of the communication pool.

Oftentimes, couples find that conversations can move rather quickly from simple disagreement to an escalated argument, which may seem disproportionate to the circumstances or subject being discussed. If you find yourself asking, "What was that all about?" or "What's the big deal?" or "Why are you so upset?" then it's a good time to slow down and examine what's really going on. Often there are issues from our past, which cause us to overreact to a situation in the present.

Let me give an illustration of what I'm talking about: Phyllis had criticized Bill. It seemed a small thing to her, yet his reaction was quick and angry. She was stunned. After a few minutes she said, "What was that all about? It seemed like an overreaction. I felt like you attacked me."

"Yeah," he said, "I don't know why I got so upset. I guess it felt like it was my mother, who always criticized me, and I was reacting to her instead of to what was said. Does that make any sense?"

"Well, at least it makes more sense than anything I can come up with."

"Well, I'm sorry," Bill said. "In the future I'll try to process things differently."

This potential argument was avoided because both parties tried hard to deal with the feelings involved. And, in the process, they were able to gain valuable insight into future communication. Sometimes the revelation as to why we overreacted to a situation may not be immediately apparent. In such cases it's important to merely recognize we overreacted and take time to process and examine what went on. In such cases, time and sincere examination of the past will often reveal the cause. The important thing is to recognize when we have overreacted and then to admit it to our spouse. If we can isolate the cause, we can come to an understanding and help prevent a recurrence. All feelings are important and should never be negated or dismissed.

Conflict is inevitable. It is not a bad thing; we simply need to learn to deal with it in a constructive manner by improving our communication skills. Forcing ourselves to explore our feelings helps us learn to better understand ourselves as well as the person with whom we are communicating. This will lead to closer and more intimate relationships. And intimacy is, after all, the goal, and the deepest level of communication.

Unfortunately, many people keep their frustrations bottled up until they explode (by which time one or both have no desire to seek counseling or outside help). If couples reach this point, many consider their circumstances beyond repair. (More about this is covered in Chapter XIII, "Advice for Troubled Times.")

And since the frustration just mentioned is one of the leading causes of anger, it is probably wise at this point to say a word or two about anger. Anger is, in and of itself, not sinful. It is what we do with the anger that can become sinful. Keep in mind, anger is like a muscle—the more we use it or exercise it, the stronger it becomes. Also, anger turned inward can cause depression. Examining our emotions is a healthy endeavor. Why am I feeling so angry? Am I frustrated about something? And if the answer to the latter question is yes, I need to examine whether I'm taking those frustrations out on someone else.

For example, I had a business partner once who said to me: "Just because you're feeling angry because you've gained weight; don't take it out on me." His words were a powerful revelation to me. He hit the nail right on the head. As a result, instead of becoming angry, I reflected on what he said and refocused on the real issue. Anger quickly turned to gratitude. Life is full of choices. We can choose to be angry, or we can choose another emotion—in this case, gratitude for a better insight into myself. Because we talked about the issue, our relationship became even stronger rather than deteriorating.

Growth in a relationship occurs proportionate with our own personal willingness to accept criticism and make required behavioral changes. Note that I said our own personal willingness, not our spouse's willingness. Personal growth depends on each one of us individually. Concentrate your efforts on changing yourself for the better, not on changing our spouse.

When communication breaks down to the extent that counseling is required, remember what has taken years to break cannot always be fixed overnight. The good news is that new quick-therapy techniques have offered some encouraging short-term results. (More is explained about these techniques in Chapter XIII, "Advice For Troubled Times.")

Nonverbal communication (not what is said, but the way it is said) is as important to a healthy relationship as verbal communication. I'm not just referring to crossed arms (a sign that the person is closed or unaccepting of what is said) or steam coming out of his ears. Nonverbal communication can also include facial expressions, volume of speech, tone of voice, or even an unexpected silence in a conversation. Perhaps the most important nonverbal communication skill of all is to know our marriage partner's heart. This is a skill that can only be acquired through intimacy over a period of time, and is distinct from mind reading, as described in Chapter IX, "Mind Games."

Let me use an example from my own life. I once became quite upset with my wife after she had reorganized our library. To be honest, the library was badly in need of reorganization. However, when I could not find a book I needed and one I had previously known exactly where to find, I became quite upset with my wife. After complaining to a good friend about my frustration with my wife, my friend pointed out he was sure my wife's actions were not intended to make my life miserable. He was certain (as I should have been) that her intent was to improve the ease with which things might be found. As I reflected on this, I clearly saw this was true. To recognize someone's intent as distinct from the result of their words or actions requires an intimate knowledge of that person, which is acquired through time and experience. This is distinct from mind reading, since it ascribes positive motives to an individual as opposed to negative ones. Yet often, as in the illustration above, we can be so focused on our own needs (the missing book) that we fail to think things through.

The thought to remember here is to try and see beyond words and actions to the actual intent, or heart, of your spouse. Take the time, and invest the effort to get to know his/her heart. Remember, your spouse loves you, that's why he/she married you!

There are a number of speech vagaries, as well, that can cause us problems, and are therefore worthy of mention here. These were originally put forth in a model by James Grinder and Richard Bandler, called the "Meta Model." The following list, as presented by them, is intended to help recognize and respond to these confusing speech patterns, and to help avoid them in our own speech.

• WHEN GATHERING INFORMATION:

BE SURE TO GET ENOUGH INFORMATION

When something important has been left out of the spoken word, confusion can result. The following exchange is an example:

"I'm really uncomfortable."

There are many ways to respond to this, but perhaps the best is to obtain more information.

For instance: "Uncomfortable about what specifically?"

• WHEN A GENERAL STATEMENT IS MADE THAT LACKS SPECIFICS:

BE SPECIFIC

An example of this might be:

"They never listen to me."

More information is obviously required. A good response to this would be:

"Who specifically never listens to you?"

This can also be true for verb usage, for example:

"She really annoys me."

Leaving us to wonder,

"How does she annoy you?"

• THE TECHNIQUE OF NOMINALIZATION IS OFTEN USED TO MISLEAD SOMEONE OR PAINT SOMEONE WITH A BROAD STROKE. IT REPRESENTS A PROCESS AS A STATIC ENTITY.

NOMINALIZATION LEADS TO MISUNDERSTANDING

For example:

"John is so insensitive."

Leaving the hearer to wonder,

"His sensing what about who, and how specifically?"

• LIMITING FACTORS

PRESUPPOSITIONS

We talked about presumptions earlier and how they can cause problems. Here we're talking about when something is assumed in another person's communications, which may, if taken for granted, cause limitations to a person's choices about the experience.

For example:

"If you knew how much I cared you wouldn't treat me that way."

(There are three presuppositions here: First, I care; Second, you treat me that way; and Third, you don't know.)

For clarification one must ask,

"How, specifically, should I know that you care? How, specifically, am I treating you? How, specifically, do you know I don't care?"

Learning to recognize and familiarize yourself with these various speech vagaries will help you to become a more effective communicator.

So, having gone through this, the longest and most important of chapters, what would I recommend you take from it as a principle?

PRINCIPLE:
Studying and improving your communication skills will pay immediate dividends to all of your personal relationships!

BIBLICAL COMMENTARY ON COMMUNICATION

Jeremiah 5:21 "Hear this, you foolish and senseless people, who have eyes but do not see, who have ears but do not hear."

This verse is reminder that God gave us eyes and ears for a reason. Let's use them as he intended.

John 8:47 "He who belongs to God hears what God says. The reason you do not hear is that you do not belong to God."

If we don't hear God, it's just possible we don't really know God. His desire is to have a personal relationship with us. This is reflected in an ongoing communication with God through the reading of His word (His way of speaking to us) and through actively praying to Him (our way of speaking to Him).

Hebrews 3:7–8 "So, as the Holy Spirit says: 'Today if you hear his voice, do not harden your hearts …'"

Equally important to an open mind is an open heart. This verse is a caution to all of us to not close our hearts, for in so doing so we hinder the work of the Spirit of God within us.

Matthew 6:14–15 "For if you forgive men when they sin against you, your heavenly Father will also forgive you. But if you do not forgive men their sins, your Father will not forgive your sins."

A stern warning to forgive as we have been forgiven, to treat others as we ourselves wish to be treated.

Ephesians 4:29–32 "Do not let any unwholesome talk come out of your mouths, but only what is helpful for building others up according to their needs, that it may benefit those who listen. And do not grieve the Holy Spirit of God, with whom you were sealed for the day of redemption. Get rid of bitterness, rage and anger, brawling and slander, along with every form of malice. Be kind and compassionate to one another, forgiving each other, just as in Christ God forgave you."

How often do things escape our lips that should never have been said? Words, once said, cannot be taken back. When we are confronted with something unflattering or even derogatory we've said about someone, an apology seldom removes the scarring that has occurred. A wise course of action: If you can't say something good, flattering, or uplifting about a person, don't say anything at all!

Colossians 3:12–14 "Therefore, as God's chosen people, holy and dearly loved, clothe yourselves with compassion, kindness, humility, goodness and patience. Bear with each other and forgive whatever grievances you may have against one another. Forgive as the Lord forgave you. And over all these virtues put on love, which binds them all together in perfect unity."

These are God's instructions. This is His plan, His agenda. Let's not replace it with our own.

James 1:19–20 "My dear brothers, take note of this: Everyone should be quick to listen, slow to speak and slow to become angry, for man's anger does not bring about the righteous life that God desires."

How often to we get this backwards: quick to speak, quick to become angry, and slow to listen?

Proverbs 1:5 "Let the wise listen and add to their learning, …"

My father once told me I could learn more with my mouth closed and my ears open than the other way around. And he was, as usual, correct.

Proverbs 12:15 "The way of a fool seems right to him, but a wise man listens to advice."

Pride is the accomplice of the fool.

Proverbs 18:13 "He who answers before listening—that is his folly and shame."

While this verse is similar in nature to the admonition of James 1:19, it is a reminder that interrupting people before they finish speaking is foolish behavior.

Chapter VII

FINANCES

The Second Leading Cause of Marital Breakdowns

Surveys reveal that finances are the second-leading cause of divorce in America today. Financial problems have always put pressure on family relationships. It is worth noting that most families in financial difficulty think generating extra income (such as the wife working) will help, but this is often not the case. In his book *How to Manage Your Money*, the late Larry Burkett points out, "Generally, the problems are caused by overspending, not insufficient income."

Take, for example, the case of Jeff and Susan. They came to us all stressed out because Jeff had been unable to find a new job and he was at the top of his pay grade in his existing job. Upon investigation, it became apparent their problem was easily resolved without Jeff having to change jobs. The couple was simply living beyond their means. A few adjustments to their spending patterns and they were soon living without the stress they had been experiencing.

The important thing to consider here is: often, additional work or a new job is not the answer. First, closely analyze and correct buying and spending habits. Perhaps one of the reasons many hold this misconception is most of us have trouble differentiating between wants, needs, and desires.

For example, food, clothing, and shelter are needs; whereas steak and lobster, *new* and *better* clothing, and a *new* or *bigger* home are wants. A luxury yacht, a beach house in the Caribbean, and a full-time maid are, for most of us, merely desires—things we will probably never be able to afford, no matter how much we want them.

Before buying anything, ask, "Do I need this or do I simply want it?" In this way we can often avoid unnecessary purchases. Remember, God has promised to provide for our needs, not for our wants or desires.

The Bible contains over 700 references to money, and nearly two-thirds of the parables Jesus told deal with the use of money. God equates our use of money with our commitment to Him. With home prices and rents soaring, it is not uncommon to find both husband and wife working at full-time jobs. With both spouses working, the stress level in a home is almost always heightened.

While financial pressures today have forced many wives into the workplace, the wisdom of this practice should be examined after children arrive on the scene. Many of the family problems that exist today occur in homes where there is no full-time, active parenting. Parents are better equipped to raise their own children than are day-care centers.

When establishing family priorities, always remember children are our most important contribution to the future. How parents raise their children and the things parents teach them will have a profound influence on the future of the world they will live in. Good financial steward-ship can be one of life's most important lessons. Sound teaching in this area will impact future generations. We need look no further than our own government to see the effects of generations of reckless spending. Perhaps, if the parents of those on both sides of the political spectrum had taught their children to be better stewards, we would not find our country is such deep debt and trying to borrow its way out.

Just as we do not live in our parents' world, our children will not live in ours. During the years in which my parents were raising children, a middle-income family might have owned a one-and-a-half-bath home with two or three bedrooms and a single-car garage. Most families at that time did not have central air conditioning, a dishwasher, or a dryer, and, if they were fortunate enough to have a clothes washer, it would have been a wringer style. Families typically owned only one car and a radio, and had no television. Microwave ovens, lawn sprinkler systems, computers, cellular phones, PDAs, MP3 players, and fax machines did not even exist. Swimming pools were a rarity.

Today, many homes have three or four baths and four or five bedrooms. Most homes come standard with a dishwasher, washer and dryer, microwave oven, and, in many parts of the country, central air conditioning, and two- and three-car garages are common. Most households now have television sets (often two or more), computers (often more than one), and cell phones. A variety of other electronic toys and devices, such as intercom systems, home theaters, and even wine cellars, can be found in many of today's more affluent households.

While it is certainly true wages have increased considerably, it is also true prices have increased substantially. Credit card usage is rampant. According to credit reporting agencies, most families today are living in debt and well beyond their means

The Federal Reserve reported that in 2007 total consumer debt in the United States was at an alarming 2.5 trillion dollars. That's nearly $8,200 in debt for every man, woman, and child in America. And that figure did not include mortgages or other loans secured by real estate. Worse yet, according to an article in the New York Times, dated January 12, 2008, this figure had risen by at least seven percent in each of the last three months of 2007. The end result of all this is financial pressure, which translates into stress. The philosophy of "buy now, pay later" has become standard practice. Many people are guilty of making purchases in anticipation of income not yet received or earned (an expected bonus check or an anticipated insurance settlement). This is no better than gambling and should be avoided.

A friend, whom I will refer to here as Len, in the expectation of a big bonus, stopped on his way home from work and bought a new washer and dryer for his wife, Ellen. Since he did not have the cash, he simply put them on his charge card, expecting to pay for them when his bonus came in. On Monday, however, Len was told the company was not going to be paying any bonuses that year and, in fact, were going to be cutting back on personnel. Though he did not lose his job, he found himself in a difficult financial situation.

In today's economy, it is more common to find couples struggling with financial problems like Len's, or even worse, than it is to find couples without financial difficulties. Avoid mortgaging your future. Live within your means. Credit cards equal debt. Never spend money you don't have. And always remember this: If you borrow money you have no ability to repay, it's the same as stealing!

Couples should discuss financial matters in some detail before marriage. For example: Which of the two will handle the money? In many cases, one spouse is much more gifted in that area. In our marriage, that would be my wife. Although I have a background in business and accounting, my wife is more fiscally conservative than I am. She knows how to set and stay within a budget (something I never learned in four years of undergraduate work and three years of graduate studies).

Engaged couples may ask, "Should we operate on a budget?" Yes, I highly recommend every couple work within a budget. A budget is nothing more than a written plan. Both husband and wife can work together to establish a budget and, once agreed upon, stick to the set budget. If one or both of the spouses has a salaried job, setting a budget is a much easier task. For couples whose income fluctuates, however, the task is more difficult. In those cases, more restraint in spending is necessary. If one month a couple earns more and spends it all, they may not be able to pay all the bills the following month. Those who need help in this area should seek the advice of someone they know who is fiscally responsible, such as an accountant or a banker. Such individuals can help when establishing a budget or in times of financial difficulty.

Many books and organizations exist that can be of great help when dealing with family finances. I recommend *How to Manage Your Money* and *Your Finances in Changing Times*, both by financial expert Larry Burkett. Many other excellent resources are available through your local library or online. Another wonderful resource is Crown Financial Ministries, a Christian organization that helps teach biblical financial principles. Many churches use Crown Financial Ministries' courses on financial stewardship. A number of organizations that operate under government charter also exist to help people in financial crisis consolidate bills and meet financial obligations. Care should be taken, however, in selecting such an organization because not all such organizations are reputable or government approved (and many of these charge for their services).

As mentioned in the previous chapter, a common problem in marriage is that one or both partners seek to avoid difficult discussions. Financial problems, by their very nature, usually fall into that category. One way to reduce this tendency is to restrict the length of such a discussion to a manageable time frame (ten to thirty minutes). Keep the time limit to a point where neither partner becomes frustrated. Another help in such situations is to set boundaries. If one of the partners is prone to exaggerate or misrepresent financial issues, require that all pertinent documents and bills be available for examination so both partners can see and agree on exactly what is being discussed.

Take, for example, the case of a couple experiencing money problems. The wife complained every time she tried to discuss finances with her husband, he found excuses to leave the room or he postponed the discussion. This situation left the wife extremely frustrated and with no apparent way to resolve the dilemma.

When a counselor confronted the husband about his avoidance behavior, the man complained his wife exaggerated financial figures. The husband would then become frustrated, and an argument would ensue. When their counselor pressed for an example, the husband said, "Last month, she accused me of spending a thousand dollars on my American Express card, and I know I didn't spend that much." The husband also complained nothing was ever resolved during their financial discussions.

The counselor recommended the following: First, the husband and wife would sit down the following morning to discuss their finances (thus answering the wife's main frustration). Second, the couple's discussion would last only fifteen minutes—a manageable time for both husband and wife. The couple agreed if more time were required they could set another date and schedule another fifteen minutes to continue the discussion. Lastly, the wife agreed to have all the bills and paperwork on hand (thereby addressing the husband's complaint of exaggerated or incorrect figures).

The results were satisfying to both parties. The American Express bill for $1,000 was correct. However, the husband had charged only $660 of the bill, and the wife had charged the balance. The couple has been meeting regularly ever since to discuss their finances. The husband has a greater appreciation of his wife's frustrations, and the wife is now comforted by her husband's participation in the process. Both have learned how to better communicate with one another. (See Chapter VI "Communication" and Chapter XIII "Advice for Troubled Times" for further discussion of this type of avoidance behavior.)

For the Christian, it is important to recognize that everything we have—our time, our talents, and our treasures—comes from God. As early as Genesis chapter four, the Bible introduces the idea of tithing, or giving back to God a portion of what He has given us. The *American Heritage Dictionary* defines "tithe" as: "a tenth part of one's annual income, paid for the support of a church." The matter of tithing is not a question of how much I should give to God, but, rather, how much of what God has given me I will keep. A Christian friend once asked his pastor, "Should I tithe on my gross income or on my net income?" The pastor replied, "That depends on whether you want a gross blessing or a net blessing." The Apostle Paul recorded in 2 Corinthians 9:7, "Each man should give what he has decided in his heart to give, not reluctantly or under compulsion, for God loves a cheerful giver." For an excellent reference work on this subject, read Randy Alcorn's book *The Treasure Principle*.

Regardless of the amount set aside for a tithe, remember God's perspective: "… Whoever sows sparingly will also reap sparingly, and whoever sows generously will also reap generously" (2 Corinthians 9:6).

> **PRINCIPLE:**
> A focus on sound financial practices, such as controlling spending (needs vs. wants) and limiting debt (tear up credit cards—if you don't have the money, you can't afford it!) will pay huge dividends for every relationship.

BIBLICAL COMMENTARY ON FINANCES AND STEWARDSHIP

Proverbs 22:9 "A generous man will himself be blessed, for he shares his food with the poor."

Good stewardship involves more than just wise spending; it involves storing up treasures in heaven as well. I have often felt more blessed by giving something of value to another than in acquiring something new for myself.

Ecclesiastes 5:10 "Whoever loves money never has money enough; whoever loves wealth is never satisfied with his income. This too is meaningless."

These words are Solomon's, a man of great wisdom, who knew great wealth and yet had discovered the shallowness of it.

Matthew 6:19–21 "Do not store up for yourselves treasures on earth where moth and rust destroy, and where thieves break in and steal. But store up for yourselves treasures in heaven, where moth and rust do not destroy, and where thieves do not break in and steal. For where your treasure is, there your heart will be also."

The martyred missionary Jim Elliot wrote in his journal, "He is no fool who gives that which he cannot keep, to gain what he cannot lose."

Matthew 6:24 "No one can serve two masters. Either he will hate the one and love the other, or he will be devoted to the one and despise the other. You cannot serve both God and Money."

As indicated in the previous verse, we put our money where our heart is.

Matthew 25:14–30 gives the parable of the talents.

Jesus teaches the importance God places on good stewardship. God expects us to use all He has given us—time, treasure, and talent—in a wise manner.

1 Timothy 6:6–10 "But godliness with contentment is great gain. For we brought nothing into the world, and we can take nothing out of it. But if we have food and clothing, we will be content with that. People who want to get rich fall into temptation and a trap and into many foolish and harmful desires that plunge men into ruin and destruction. For the love of money is a root of all kinds of evil. Some people, eager for money, have wandered from the faith and pierced themselves with many griefs."

Just as hearses do not pull U-Hauls and funeral clothing has no pockets, we are reminded here that we cannot take anything with us. The love of money and material possessions can be a great trap. That is why Jesus said it was harder for a wealthy man to enter heaven than for a camel to pass through the eye of a needle (Matthew 19:24). Yet even this is possible with God.

2 Corinthians 9:6–7 "Remember this: Whoever sows sparingly will also reap sparingly, and whoever sows generously will also reap generously. Each man should give what we have decided in our heart to give, not reluctantly or under compulsion, for God loves a cheerful giver."

A great gauge of where we are spiritually is usually what we give to God and to the needy. We do well to remember it all belongs to God. So the question is not, "How much should I give?" but rather, "How much should I give back?"

Hebrews 13:5 "Keep yourselves free from the love of money and be content with what you have, because God has said, 'Never will I leave you; never will I forsake you.'"

Greed and avarice are each other's best friends, but they need not be our best friends.

Chapter VIII

FIGHTING FAIR—
THE UPSIDE OF ARGUMENTS

In a marriage, even the best of marriages, disagreements are inevitable. As pointed out in the chapter on communication, disagreements arise out of differing opinions. Try as we might, we cannot always agree. The secret, then, is to learn to disagree agreeably.

Many couples marry expecting their marriage relationship to proceed as trouble-free as the courtship. But, remember, most of us are on our best behavior when courting someone. Still, many couples go quite a while without having any significant bumps in the road. Rest assured, however, somewhere in the future lurks an ugly confrontation. Expect it. Then deal with it. Don't react as if the world has ended.

How do we deal with conflict? The answer to this question can reveal the success or failure of a marriage. Dr John Gottman and a team of researchers from the University of Washington have been studying marriages for over twenty years. Their research has shown there are significant indicators that point to either the success or failure of relationships. In his book *The Marriage Clinic: A Scientifically Based Marriage Therapy*, Dr. Gottman states, "There are four patterns, which can emerge when conflict occurs. Each paves the way for the next until the relationship is destroyed." They are, in order of least destructive to most destructive: Criticism, Contempt, Defensiveness, and Stonewalling." Let's examine each one of these and see how we can avoid being trapped by destructive behavior.

1. Criticism. Some time ago, there was a bestselling book entitled *The One Minute Manager*, by Kenneth Blanchard and Spencer Johnson. This book made a crucial point: There is a significant difference between criticizing an individual (be it worker, child, or spouse) and criticizing the *behavior* of that individual. When we criticize an individual, the person rejects that criticism because he/she feels personally attacked. If, however, we make the distinction between the individual and the behavior, he/she can accept the criticism, release the behavior, and move on.

An illustration of this would be: "John, you're usually such a responsible guy and a great businessman, but when you spend money as recklessly as you just did on that new car it truly disappoints me. I know you know better than that. You usually exercise good judgment."

Contrast this example with a more common, yet incorrect, method of criticizing the individual: "John, how could you be so stupid? Buying a car now was just idiotic!"

Note: In the first illustration, John is more likely to change his behavior. In the second, (in addition to a rejection of the criticism) an argument will likely ensue. More importantly, perhaps, is the likelihood John will continue his irresponsible behavior.

There is a fine line between criticism of a person and criticism of that person's behavior, yet the results of such criticism are usually quite dramatic. Strive to criticize a specific behavior rather than the person. This technique requires practice, but will pay huge dividends toward building a healthier relationship. One way to examine progress in this area is to notice whether criticisms are having the desired affect or are simply falling on deaf ears.

2. Contempt. What separates contempt from criticism? According to Dr. Gottman, it's the *intention* to insult and psychologically abuse a person. That's what makes it so crucial we think before we speak. Our intent should be to help the other person, not to put them down.

It's also essential we not form bad habits. (Remember, it takes a time to develop a habit, but an even longer time to break a habit.) One bad habit that is extremely destructive to relationships is to push your partner's hot buttons. It's easy over time to discover certain things we say or do that can set our spouse off very quickly. Remember, *contempt* is the opposite of *respect*. If we respect our spouse, we will not want to invoke anger or any other negative response.

To illustrate, let's examine the following example: In the middle of a heated argument, John shouts, "You're just like your mother." This not only implies there is something wrong with John's wife, but, additionally, her mother is just as bad. The disagreement escalates from criticism to contempt. Now, totally angered, his wife strikes back, "Well I know how difficult it must be for you, coming from the *perfect* family that you do." The danger in crossing these fine lines is that it's very easy to do, and crossing one line makes it easier to cross the next until the relationship is in shambles.

3. Defensiveness. Dr. Gottman says, "Defending ourselves comes so naturally. 'How can it be destructive?' you might reasonably ask. The main problem with defensiveness is that it escalates rather than resolves conflicts. Every time we deny responsibility we make it someone else's problem." We're, in effect, saying, "It's not my fault; it's yours." An excellent technique, and one you may not have tried, is simply to admit it's your fault: "You're right, I messed up. What would you like me to do?" You can even say this when you don't think you're wrong. Crazy? I don't think so. The results are always amazing, and it stops the escalation.

Perhaps the best way to illustrate this point is to demonstrate both a right and a wrong way to handle a situation. First let's look at the wrong way: "Why is it my fault? You live here too. Why am I always the one who gets blamed?" Now let's look at the opposite way and see if that doesn't sound better: "I'm sorry, dear. What can I do to make it right?"

Accepting responsibility is healthier for relationships than denial and defensiveness. Remember, It's better to be righteous than right.

4. Stonewalling. What exactly is stonewalling and why is it so destructive? Stonewalling, according to Dr. Gottman, is literally refusing to interact It's giving up. It's saying, "I can't win with you, so why try?" It's withdrawing. The dangers, Dr. Gottman points out, are significant. We have already addressed the problems of withdrawal in Chapter VII on finances and in Chapter VI on communication. When one partner pushes and one partner withdraws, it usually leads to frustration and ultimately to a total breakdown of communication. Most often, it is the man who withdraws; however, it can be either spouse, and it is dangerous.

Let's look at how this might play out in a real life scenario.

Wife: "Don't just sit there, say something."

Husband: Simply shrugs disgustedly.

Wife: "Oh, so now you're going to shut up and leave the whole mess in my lap?" Husband: Gets up and leaves the room.

The lesson to be learned here, and it's an important one, is to interact! Growth comes out of conflict. A refusal to engage is a refusal to grow in a relationship.

Almost every husband and wife exhibits one or more of these behaviors from time to time during the course of their relationship. The real danger is in letting them become habits. Learn to recognize them and to avoid them.

FIGHT FAIR. We've already talked briefly about "hot buttons." Don't use them. If you catch yourself using them, and, believe me, you'll know when you've pushed one, stop and apologize immediately. Clear the air. Chances are excellent you need a break in the conversation at this point anyway. Don't talk down to your wife or husband. Remember, you love each other—that's why you married. You are a team, both on the same side. Your spouse should not be the enemy, but rather your best friend. You need each other. Don't insult your spouse, and don't clam up. No matter how rough the water in the deep end of the communication pool, you'll find effective communication leads to a stronger and healthier relationship. Often, prayer can be an effective way to "cool off" when an argument begins to heat up. It has worked well for my wife and I.

As has already been pointed out, relationships will always, given enough time, involve conflict. So, instead of avoiding conflict, learn how to deal with it when it occurs. There are four different styles of conflict resolution. Each of us employs one or more of these as a predominant style: 1) Avoidance, 2) Accommodation, 3) Collaboration, and 4) Compromise.

When the avoidance style is used within the framework of a marriage, one partner is usually more aggressive, while the other tends to retreat. Over time, as one pushes and the other retreats, one partner will eventually tire of pushing or retreating and may want to end the relationship. Either party can ease the tension and save the relationship. See Chapter VII, "Finances," for an example of this type of behavior.

Sometimes when in the midst of a heated argument, one spouse chooses to simply walk out of the house, while the other party is left to steam and stew in a feeling of helplessness. If this pattern is repeated (stonewalling, as discussed above, occurs), and if the spouse who feels helpless believes the problem will never be addressed or resolved, the relationship will often end in separation or divorce. It should be noted, some people retreat when a situation gets too heated. Retreat can be a means of cooling off or clarifying thinking, or perhaps to simply take time out to pray. If this is the case, the retreating party should explain to the other person that he or she is not avoiding the issue, but will return to discuss it at another time. If possible, set a specific time and a time limit for the discussion (ten to thirty minutes), and establish guidelines or boundaries for the discussion.

Let's examine how this might work in a real-life situation. Pam and John were no exceptions to the passive/aggressive pattern common to many relationships. Pam tended to be the aggressor, while Tom (disliking fights) tended to simply leave the room or even the house if necessary. This "fight or flight" tendency is a familiar reaction in relationships. Usually one person pushes and another retreats. Either party can stop this pattern. The pusher can stop pushing, or the one retreating can cease retreating. If the pattern continues unchecked, one party will often give up and seek to end the relationship. In this case, Tom finally stopped running and stayed to talk through the problem. The important thing to remember is to not avoid potential problems—talk through them!

USE ARGUMENTS AS A LEARNING EXPERIENCE. Always remember that conflict is essential to growth. The Apostle Paul said in 1 Corinthians 7:28, "… those who marry will face many troubles in this life …" Jesus likewise promised in John 16:33, "In this world you will have trouble …" And James said: "Consider it pure joy, my brothers, whenever you face trials of many kinds, because you know that the testing of your faith develops perseverance. Perseverance must finish its work so that you may be mature and complete, not lacking anything" (James 1:2–3). Trials strengthen us. They help us grow. No one truly enjoys going through difficult times; however, many of us look back at trials in our life and recognize they were in some ways a blessing. In his book, *The Good Life*, Chuck Colson says, "What we strive for can often be what we least need. What we fear most can turn out to be our greatest blessing." This quote is from a man who knows what it means to suffer trials, and also from a man who knows what James meant about finding joy in trials.

Use arguments as a means to grow in your relationship. Learn from them. Ask yourself questions such as, "How can I avoid getting into this type of argument the next time?" or "What could I have done or said that would have been more appropriate?" Try never to waste a good argument without taking something of value from it. Real growth in a relationship occurs best when we learn through our mistakes.

FORGIVENESS. It would be remiss to talk about arguments and not to talk about forgiveness. Learning to forgive is, perhaps, one of life's most important lessons. It is possible, if not probable, you know someone who struggles with unforgiveness. If so, you've seen how damaging this can be, not just to relationships but, rather, to the person who has refused to let go of some issue or hurt, either real or perceived.

Forgiving someone is not the same as forgetting; nor does it mean that a relationship is fully restored. Depending on the depth of the hurt, it may take considerable time for trust to be rebuilt and a relationship restored. Yet to remain angry and refuse to forgive someone causes pain to ourselves. Often, the other party remains unaware we are hurt or angry. Why then must we forgive?

God commands us to forgive in Matthew 6:14–15, "For if you forgive men when they sin against you, your heavenly Father will also forgive you. But if you do not forgive men their sins, your Father will not forgive your sins." Also God connects forgiveness with love in 1 Corinthians chapter 13 where it says, "Love ... keeps no record of wrongs." When we hold past events against someone, it's as if we are keeping a file on them. Then, we can drag out the file whenever we want and use the file against them. Don't store this destructive file in your memory banks! Hit "delete" and send those files to the trash. Keeping such files hurts the one keeping them, as well as the one they are used against. The most often recommended, and seemingly the most effective, way to do this is to pray for the person you're angry with. It is not easy, but do it for your own good.

An excellent book dealing with forgiveness was mentioned in Chapter V, *70 x 7 and Beyond: Mystery of the Second Chance* by Monty Christensen.

What then would be the most important principle we might take from this chapter?

PRINCIPLE:
Be alert to the following symptoms of a deteriorating relationship:
1) criticism of your spouse as a person rather than criticism of behavior; 2) showing contempt for your spouse; 3) becoming defensive in your relationship, and 4) stonewalling or refusal to interact with your spouse. Recognize the symptoms, and immediately take steps to correct them!

BIBLICAL COMMNTARY ON ARGUMENTS AND CRITICISM

Numbers 14:18 "The LORD is slow to anger, abounding in love and forgiving sin and rebellion...."

If we are looking for an example of a proper response, we need look no further.

Proverbs 15:1 "A gentle answer turns away wrath, but a harsh word stirs up anger."

Goodness is returned in kind; therefore it should be no surprise that our hostility would most likely lead to anger.

Proverbs 29:11 "A fool gives vent to his anger, but a wise man keeps himself under control."

Self-control, a fruit of the Spirit, is alluded to here.

Proverbs 30:33 "For as churning the milk produces butter, and as twisting the nose produces blood, so stirring up anger produces strife."

Certain actions will always produce certain results. Therefore, it benefits us to practice those actions that produce good results and avoid those actions that produce unfavorable results.

Ephesians 4:26–27 "'In your anger do not sin': Do not let the sun go down while you are still angry, and do not give the devil a foothold."

There is more wisdom here than you might imagine. My father's advice was simply, "Don't go to bed mad." For one thing, you don't usually sleep too well, and, for another, you usually wake up angry and wreck another entire day. You will find that apologies are not too painful, and agreement is usually easier to come by after an apology. Apologize, even when you don't feel you've done anything wrong. In almost every instance, you can say, "I'm sorry I've upset you." Avoid, however, any disingenuous apology, such as: "I'm sorry, but you know I'm right," or "I'm sorry, but you just don't get it." Remember, the word "but" erases anything that precedes it.

Talk about why you're feeling angry. In the end, you'll not only sleep better, you'll also bring about growth in your relationship. Lose the ideas that it's a weakness to give in and apologize, or that you're right and they're wrong. These ideas are lies from Satan, who would have you believe you are always in the right. Work, rather, at understanding why you feel you're right, and try to get your spouse to explain why he/she feels as he/she does. It will be uncomfortable to explore your feelings, especially if you have not had much experience at it. But work at it. All meaningful relationships take effort. And the great night's sleep you get will make it all worthwhile. Making up is the best part of any disagreement.

1 Corinthians 13:4-8 "Love is patient, love is kind. It does not envy, it does not boast, it is not proud. It is not rude, it is not self-seeking, it is not easily angered, it keeps no record of wrongs. Love does not delight in evil, but rejoices with the truth. It always protects, always trusts, always hopes, always perseveres. Love never fails...."

This is the portion of the love passage that deals with anger, keeping a record of wrongs, rudeness, etc. As pointed out in the chapter on love, this is a great checklist for the kind of love you are showing to your spouse.

James 1:19–20 "My dear brothers, take note of this: Everyone should be quick to listen, slow to speak and slow to become angry, for man's anger does not bring about the righteous life that God desires."

A reminder that listening trumps speaking.

Chapter IX

MIND GAMES

Expectations, Assumptions, Assigning Motives, and Other Dangerous Games

This section is closely related to Chapter VI on communication. I have entitled this chapter "Mind Games" simply because the five items discussed here are hazardous mental games in which couples sometimes engage. They are, in the order discussed: Unrealistic Expectations, Sweeping Generalities, Assumptions, Jumping to Conclusions, and Assigning Motives/Mind Reading.

• Expectations

Expectations fall into two categories: realistic and unrealistic. We all have expectations, but it's the unrealistic ones that get us into trouble. We must constantly ask ourselves, "Is the expectation I have realistic?"

Let's illustrate with the following example: I expect my wife to remember I'm going to hunting camp next week, despite the fact that I set up this hunting date a year ago with my friends. I may (or may not) have mentioned it to her at that time, but have definitely not mentioned it since. Realistic or unrealistic? Obviously, this would be an unrealistic expectation. I must remind my wife as soon as I remember it (hopefully, not the day before I leave).

Let's take a look at another example: I expect my wife to keep the house reasonably clean and presentable. Realistic or unrealistic? Generally realistic, depending of whether or not my wife works outside the home, her health, and also on what roles we have agreed in advance to accept. It could also depend on whether or not I am an obsessive compulsive or whether or not we share the same view of "reasonably clean and presentable." So, the determination of whether or not an expectation is realistic or unrealistic can often be quite subjective.

Still another example, this one also somewhat subjective: I expect my wife to remember our anniversary. Would this be realistic or unrealistic? In my particular case, this would be unrealistic. My wife and I both have a history (going back twenty years) of forgetting our anniversary.

In each instance, when we expect something, we will be disappointed if that expectation is not met. Disappointments usually lead to disagreements. As a result, it is important to not only examine our expectations, but also to discuss them. In this way, we will learn over time to be disappointed less, and we will learn not to set ourselves up for disappointment.

The main point is to guard against unrealistic expectations. When angry, always ask if the anger is the result of an unrealistic expectation. Remember, also, the difference between realistic and unrealistic can often be quite subjective. Since this is not usually black and white, it may be necessary to get more than one opinion on the matter (a best friend or mother-in-law may not be the best choices for a second opinion—this would, of course, depend on the objectivity of the best friend or the mother-in-law).

One of the more common problems my wife and I encounter when counseling couples is the discovery they have never talked at length about their expectations. Couples should thoroughly discuss their expectations before entering into a marriage. Everyone has expectations, and these expectations can vary greatly.

Important expectations to consider before marriage would be: regarding family, such as how often to visit parents or how many children the couple wishes to have. Couples also have varying financial expectations, such as how soon to buy a house or what level of income is sufficient. Career expectations, such as is one spouse willing to move if a job opportunity for the other presents itself? Or, how does the couple feel about the wife working? Everyone has different spiritual expectations too, such as if children will be raised attending church, or which denomination, or where children will learn their values. Additionally, there are social expectations, such as how often to eat out, who will be included in a close circle of friends, etc. Individuals also have varying physical expectations, such as how often to make love and what sexual acts might be considered acceptable or unacceptable. The list goes on.

As much as possible, these expectations should be discussed prior to marriage. If the couple has major differences (and often they do), these differences need to be addressed before the wedding. If the differences seem too difficult to resolve, it may be necessary to consult a counselor or other objective third party.

To illustrate just how important this can be, let me give the following example. Steve married a much younger woman. For Steve, it was his second marriage. He had two children from his first marriage and didn't really want any more. Natalie, on the other hand, wanted children badly. Although they had discussed the subject briefly, Steve felt it was no big deal and proceeded to have a vasectomy without telling her. After the marriage, Natalie was appalled. She had felt they were on the same page, and had expected a family together.

If your counselor doesn't bring this up, take it upon yourselves to discuss these important expectations before the marriage. The longer the list of expectations you discuss and resolve, the fewer surprises and arguments you will have later.

• Sweeping Generalities

We must be careful in our speech. All too often, we are prone to generalize or use universal terms such as *all* or *never*. Such speech habits often lead to disagreements.

95

For example, we often hear someone say, "You never listen to me." A response to such a far-reaching statement might be something to the effect, "That's just not true" (denial). While a proper response might sound more like this: "I *never* listen to you? How do you know I *never* listen to you?"

It is best to avoid words such as never, always, every, and all. Train yourself to respond properly to the use of these words by others. Strive for clarification without denying the feelings the person has.

Let's use this example to illustrate this point: Our spouse says, "You never listen to me." Rather than hearing a legitimate level of frustration because we did not hear what was just said, we are apt to deny any credence to the statement, and dismiss it with a simple but angry response, such as, "That's a ridiculous thing to say," or "That's simply not true."

• **Assumptions**

Like expectations, assumptions can, and usually do, set us up for disappointments. Unlike expectations, assumptions are almost always dangerous. The danger lies in the very nature of an assumption; it is something we do not know and yet have accepted as true. Assumptions are, therefore, based on a presumption of knowledge—we have presumed to know something we do not.

Let us take, for example, a newly married couple. Each assumes the other is fiscally responsible. Imagine the shock when a husband (or wife) finds out that his (or her) new life partner is an out-of-control spender or an addicted gambler.

Someone once said that to assume makes an "ass" out of "u" and "me." Assuming certainly sets us up for disappointment.

Though assumptions are closely allied to expectations, there is a difference. For example: My wife says she will pick me up from work at 6:00 PM because my car is in the shop. I have an expectation this will happen. Such an expectation should, of course, be tempered by a history of my wife's timeliness, by the realization she may receive an important long-distance phone call just as she is about to leave the house, or by the possibility she might incur unexpected heavy traffic on the way to my office. It is entirely different if I tell my wife in the morning that I'm dropping off my car for repairs and *assume* she understands she is supposed to pick me up. Such an assumption really means I expect her to read my mind.

It is always best not to assume anything. Communicate your thoughts and feelings with words.

• **Jumping to Conclusions**

The practice of jumping to conclusions is closely associated with assumptions. Frequently, the practice of jumping to conclusions can cause us to sprain our relationships. Let's take a look at an example:

John comes home from work late one night with lipstick on his cheek and greets his wife, Mary, who is in the midst of preparing dinner. His wife, upon noting the late hour and the lipstick, concludes he has been with another woman.

Scenario 1 (not recommended)

Having reached this conclusion, she makes inappropriate use of the skillet in her hand.

Scenario 2 (recommended)

Mary says, "John, you're late, and you have lipstick on your cheek. Would you care to explain?"

John then replies, "Oh, I stopped off at Mom's house, and we got involved in a long discussion about her health. She kissed me goodbye when I left."

Not satisfied, Mary chooses to call John's mom and verify the visit, which, it turns out, was true.

In a subsequent discussion, John tells Mary he is disappointed and hurt she did not believe him and called to verify his story. Mary replies simply, "Well, be glad I did, because my first impulse was to put that skillet over your head." (See also Chapter VI on communication and Chapter V on trust.)

Jumping to conclusions is a very close relative to making assumptions, and, although jumping to conclusions is a bit more extreme, both should be avoided. It is far safer and more productive to ask questions and to act on actual knowledge.

• Assigning Motives

Assigning motives seems to be a popular pastime among people today. I hear it almost everywhere I go. "She did that to hurt me." "They just wanted to aggravate us." "They only did that because they're jealous." I have heard an individual accuse another person of lying, when in fact that person simply was ignorant of the facts and was reporting them as he thought them to be. I have heard one person accuse a best friend of doing something to hurt her, when that was the furthest thought from the friend's mind.

Assigning motives, like assumptions, is to pretend to know someone else's mind. No matter how well we know someone, we cannot know his or her mind or motives unless we are told them. To attempt to do this is presumptuous and irresponsible. It is best to never ascribe motives to the actions of others.

Often I find people combining any number of these mind games. For example, I was called upon to arbitrate a dispute between an employer and an employee. The dispute arose when the employee, *expecting* to be gainfully employed for some time into the future, had recently purchased a new home. The employer, however, under threat of an impending lawsuit, elected to declare bankruptcy. Thus, the employee found himself with a new mortgage and no job. Accusations began to fly. Soon both parties were hopelessly embroiled in a battle. The employee alleged (in fact, *jumped to the conclusion*) that the employer was being dishonest and disingenuous. The employee accused his employer of moving a large motorhome from the front of his property to the rear of his property in an effort to hide it from creditors (assigning a motive).

The employer explained he had placed the motorhome at the front of his property with a "For Sale" sign in the window, and then had removed the sign and moved it to the back of the property (effectively taking it off the market) until clear ownership—personal or business—could be established by the court. Upon hearing this, and with no real knowledge of the validity of the claim, the employee called the employer a liar (assumption, jumping to conclusion, and mind reading), thereby escalating the argument.

Unfortunately, most of us are guilty of playing one or more of these mind games in the conduct of our everyday lives. Only by knowing about these sorts of games and the dangers entailed in their use can we avoid them. Remember this thought: "A wise person knows or keeps silent; a foolish person who does not know, guesses." This is the same thought as expressed in the following saying: "Better to remain silent and be thought a fool, than to open your mouth and remove all doubt."

What then is the most important thought or principle to take from this chapter?

> **PRINCIPLE:**
> **Avoidance of unrealistic expectations, assumptions, sweeping generalities, and jumping to conclusions will enhance all your personal relationships.**

BIBLICAL COMMENTARY ON MIND GAMES

Proverbs 16:2 "All a man's ways seem innocent to him, but motives are weighed by the LORD."

It is always good to remember God knows our motives. We may fool ourselves, or even others, but God is never deceived.

Isaiah 26:3 "You will keep in perfect peace him whose mind is steadfast, because he trusts in you."

Peace comes to those who trust in God.

Jeremiah 17:10 "I the Lord search the heart and examine the mind ..."

Similar to Proverbs 16 above—God knows our heart,

Haggai 1:9 "'You expected much, but see, it turned out to be little....'"

This verse deals with false expectations and the ensuing disappointments.

Matthew 7:1 "Do not judge, or you too will be judged."

We are reminded in Scripture that God will one day judge us, and especially on those points at which we judge others. Just as we are admonished to be slow to speak, we should also be slow to judge.

Romans 14:13 "Therefore let us stop passing judgment on one another. Instead, make up your mind not to put any stumbling block or obstacle in your brother's way."

This is another verse dealing with passing judgment.

1 Corinthians 4:5 "Therefore judge nothing before the appointed time; wait till the Lord comes. He will bring to light what is hidden in darkness and will expose the motives of men's hearts...."

When we attempt to judge the motives of another person, we are, in affect, entering a guessing game, for no one but God knows another's true heart.

James 4:1 "What causes fights and quarrels among you? Don't they come from your desires that battle within you?"

Have you ever noticed that when you're angry with yourself on some point, there is a tendency to take out your ill feelings on those closest to you? The Greek word used in this verse for "desires" is the word from which we derive our word "hedonism." Hedonism is simply the idea that pleasure is the most important thing. So, there's an element of "it's all about me" to this verse.

Chapter X

ASSIGNING ROLES

In the twenty-first century, couples must be careful about assuming traditional roles. By this, I mean assuming the wife will be the home-maker and the man the breadwinner.

To illustrate this point let me use an example of some personal acquaintances: The wife is a physician, and the husband is a realtor. Both practiced their professions until the wife became pregnant. Upon the birth of their first child, and after some discussion, they decided on accepting nontraditional roles. The wife's earning potential far out-weighed that of her husband. Since they both agreed one parent should be home with the child, they elected for the husband to be the stay-at-home caregiver. The wife continued her medical practice. This has worked well for both of them. In this day and age, "Mr. Mom" is becom-ing more common than in past generations.

In Chapter VII "Finances," I briefly discussed that couples should not assume the husband will handle the finances; rather, the couple should evaluate the background, training, spending habits, and overall financial responsibility of each partner. My wife, Phyllis, and I have alternated over the years. In the early years, she was more financially responsible, and therefore assumed responsibility for all our bill paying. My wife came from a very conservative family background. This was not so in my case. While my father was somewhat conservative, my mother was a world-class shopper. As a result, both my sister and I followed suit. Thanks to my wife's patient example, I have been able to correct my careless spending habits. Later, as the job of bill paying became burdensome for her (and as I learned to be more fiscally responsible), I assumed that role. Additionally, I switched to online bill paying, and I am much more computer literate than my wife.

In my first marriage, it was my practice to come home from work, flop on the couch, and assume I had done my work for the day. Following my divorce, however, I was forced to fulfill the role of both mother and father. I soon discovered the truth of the saying, "a mother's work is never done." Between cleaning house, preparing meals, doing laundry, preparing school lunches, etc., after only a short time, I wondered how any woman could possibly do the job single-handedly.

Today, my wife enjoys the fruits of my learning. We divide household chores and responsibilities in a way that works for us both. My wife helps me with yard work, and I in turn, help her with housework (though she tells me I am not very good at it). This approach has served to bring us closer together. We both appreciate the contribution each makes to the marriage.

Many couples choose to follow traditional roles. That's perfectly fine. The best thing, however, is to talk about this before getting married and to develop a reality-based plan. As with any plan, if it doesn't work, change it. There is, however, a danger here; and the danger is in *assuming* the husband won't mind if the wife works outside the home, or that he will handle the finances, etc. In Chapter IX, "Mind Games," I discuss the dangers of assumptions. Be flexible. Work together as a team. Do not assume anything when it comes to the "who will do what?" in a relationship.

Today's cost of living and the economic realities of the modern world have forced many mothers to work outside the home. This has caused countless children to grow up in homes where both parents work (if they are fortunate enough to live in a two-parent household). The results of this reality can be seen in a number of unfortunate indices.

Take for example, teen suicides—the rate has skyrocketed in recent years. Many teenagers report feeling unloved. Another example might be the rise in the number of abortions. Am I saying working mothers are the only cause or even the major cause in this rise? Certainly not; however, I can remember from my own youth dating a girl whose parents both worked. Many days we found ourselves alone in their home after school, and, while nothing unseemly ever happened, we live today in a different age. Morality seems to be a forgotten concept.

Still another illustration might be the tremendous rise in drug use found in schools across America. While some may argue there is no cause-and-effect relationship in these issues, I would be forced to disagree. Anyone who has counseled children can report with some authority the relationship between limited parenting and behavioral problems in children. My point is simply that couples ought to seriously consider the impact of their decisions. For example, some questions to ask are: "Am I placing more importance on my lifestyle than I am on my children's futures?" Or, "Have I considered how my decision to work may affect my children?" I realize this may be an oversimplification and that in some cases there may be no option except for both parents to work. In any case, parents should consider carefully the impact of their decisions once children are a part of the equation.

For those just considering marriage, this is not an issue that needs to be dealt with immediately, but rather a future consideration. Still, it would be helpful to discuss before children come along. It is all too easy for us to become selfish in our thinking. When this happens, we begin to rationalize all of our decisions.

What then can we conclude is the major application or principle we can draw from this chapter?

> PRINCIPLE:
> Marriage is a team sport; develop a team mentality and
> work ethic in your home.

BIBLICAL COMMENTARY ON ROLES

Genesis 3:16 "To the woman he said: 'I will greatly increase your pains in childbearing; with pain you will give birth to children. Your desire will be for your husband, and he will rule over you.'"

This verse is often misunderstood. The reference to the husband "ruling" over the wife is a reference to God's order of things. It does not imply man is superior to woman. For just as Christ is the head over man, and God is the head over Christ, there is no inference that Christ is any way inferior to God. Without order there is quite simply anarchy. In God's order of things we are never required to do anything that denies Christ. We are only under obligation to obey our government as long as it is not in contrast to God's instructions. Christ said, "Give to Caesar what is Caesar's and give to God what is God's" (Matthew 22:21).

Genesis 3:17-19 "To Adam he said, 'Because you listened to your wife and ate from the tree about which I commanded you, "You must not eat of it," Cursed is the ground because of you; through painful toil you will eat of it all the days of your life. It will produce thorns and thistles for you, and you will eat the plants of the field. By the sweat of your brow you will eat your food until you return to the ground, since from the ground you were taken ...'"

Adam's original sin and disobedience introduced death, pain, and suffering into the world. We have to work hard for our food and struggle through life.

Proverbs 12:4 "A wife of noble character is her husband's crown, but a disgraceful wife is like decay in his bones."

This verse is similar to Proverbs 32:10, and simply points out that each of us can be a blessing or a curse to our spouse. Which one would you rather be? Which one would God have you be?

Proverbs 31:10–12 "A wife of noble character who can find? She is worth more than rubies. Her husband has full confidence in her and lacks nothing of value. She brings him good, not harm, all the days of her life."

As a Christian husband with a Christian wife, this is one of my favorite verses in the Bible; for truly my wife is worth far more to me than rubies. She has my full confidence, and she is truly the joy of my life. (There is no implication here that we do not have major disagreements from time to time or that we never fight.)

1 Corinthians 7:3 "The husband should fulfill his marital duty to his wife, and likewise the wife to her husband."

Reference is also made to this verse in Chapter XII on sexual relations. It deals with a specific portion of the roles of husband and wife in marriage.

1 Corinthians 11:3 "Now I want you to realize that the head of every man is Christ, and the head of woman is man, and the head of Christ is God."

This verse also deals with the headship issue, as does Genesis 3:16 explained above.

Ephesians 5:22-33 "Wives, submit to your husbands as to the Lord. For the husband is the head of the wife as Christ is the head of the church, his body, of which he is the Savior. Now as the church submits to Christ, so also wives should submit to their husbands in everything. Husbands, love your wives, just as Christ loved the church and gave himself up for her to make her holy, cleansing her by the washing with water through the word, and to present her to himself as a radiant church, without stain or wrinkle or any other blemish, but holy and blameless. In this same way, husbands ought to love their wives as their own bodies. He who loves his wife loves himself. After all, no one ever hated his own body, but he feeds and cares for it, just as Christ does the church—for we are members of his body. 'For this reason a man will leave his father and mother and be united to his wife, and the two will become one flesh.' This is a profound mystery—but I am talking about Christ and the church. However, each one of you also must love his wife as he loves himself, and the wife must respect her husband."

These key verses deal with roles and responsibilities of a man and a woman in the marriage relationship. This is touched on in the Chapter IV on love as it relates to the issues of responsibilities, but is here referred to because of its reference to roles.

1 Timothy 2:9 "I also want women to dress modesty, with decency and propriety, not with braided hair or gold or pearls or expensive clothes, but with good deeds appropriate for women who profess to worship God."

The reference in this verse to proper dress for women, although relating to Bible times and customs, still has validity for today in terms of propriety and good judgment. When dealing with issues of customs of the times, we must be careful to be neither too dismissive nor too legalistic. For instance, although the issue of homosexuality was addressed under the Levitical codes dealing with customs such as cleanliness and morality in Old Testament times, it does not allow us to dismiss the fact that God specifically told Moses the practice was 'detestable' (Leviticus 18:22). If the practice of a man lying with a man was detestable to God then, it is still detestable to Him now. God may allow change in customs of dress, but not on issues of morality.

1 Peter 3:1 "Wives, in the same way be submissive to your husbands so that, if any of them do not believe the word, they may be won over without words by the behavior of their wives."

This verse addresses the issue of a believing spouse remaining married to a nonbelieving spouse, with the purpose of winning the unbeliever to the Lord. Remember, you may be the only view of Christ that some people may ever see.

Titus 2:2-7 "Teach the older men to be temperate, worthy of respect, self-controlled, and sound in faith, in love and in endurance. Likewise, teach the older women to be reverent in the way they live, not to be slanderers or addicted to much wine, but to teach what is good. Then they can train the younger women to love their husbands and children, to be self-controlled and pure, to be busy at home, to be kind, and to be subject to their husbands, so that no one will malign the word of God. Similarly, encourage the young men to be self-controlled. In everything set them an example by doing what is good...."

God's plan is for older people to teach the younger people and to set examples for them as to proper ways to live. This does not mean that older people cannot learn valuable lessons from the young, or that the examples older people sets are always good examples. These verses simply list specific good examples God desires us to set for those younger. We need to be discerning in terms of what we pick up from our elders and what we pass on to our children.

Chapter XI

IN-LAWS/OUT-LAWS

One of the first things I usually do when counseling couples who are contemplating a life together is to obtain a family history. This history takes a look at parents, grandparents, brothers, sisters, aunts, uncles, previous spouses (if any), and children by previous marriage (if any). It looks at past history of abuses (either physical, emotional, or substance) and any history of physical or mental illness that might be hereditary. A family history is necessary so couples may enter into marriage with a fuller knowledge of the issues that will face them in their new life together. Surprises (unless they are for birthdays, anniversaries, or other similar occasions) should generally be kept to a minimum in a healthy marriage.

As an illustration of why this is so important, consider the case of Mary and John, who were married but had never had any premarital counseling or an evaluation of their family histories. After their first child began school, one of their son's teachers reported suspected child abuse after discovering bruises on the boy and questioning him. John, it was later discovered, had a history of abuse by his own father. John's father had, in turn, been abused by John's grandfather. If a personal history had revealed this earlier, it could have been discussed and perhaps avoided.

It is helpful for couples to understand that parents have a distinct influence on their children. It is not uncommon for children who were abused to become abusive themselves. While this is not always so, it is necessary to look at these issues in some detail before marriage. In similar fashion, people with a history of alcohol abuse need to be alert to the potential for future problems. ACOA (adult children of alcoholics) often reflect certain tendencies, which can prove harmful to relationships.

For example, in an alcoholic home there is a great secret, which family members feel pressure to keep. This usually results in lying in an effort to keep the secret. Often, lying then becomes a life pattern for the ACOA.

In his book *Family Ministry: Family Life Through the Church*, Dr. Charles M. Sell points to four additional problems that occur with ACOAs. They are: problems with trusting people, problems with handling feelings, being depressed, and being over-responsible (which can lead to codependency). Dr. Sell goes on to point out, "They tend to be compulsive about many things." He says one expert claims ACOAs have the following tendencies: "They overachieve, overeat, over-exercise, and overspend." The point here being that many issues can arise in families with a history of alcohol or substance abuse, and they are best addressed before entering a marriage relationship.

Likewise, sibling rivalries can also become unhealthy issues after marriage, and the potential for such issues is best addressed in advance of marriage. Anticipating and dealing with such concerns will usually result in avoidance of future problems.

For example, during one premarital counseling session, we were discussing family history with a young couple who saw no potential problems, when suddenly a major disagreement erupted over how they would raise their children. The bride-to-be said she loved her future husband's parents, but she would certainly not raise her children the way they had raised him. "What's wrong with the way they raised me?" the husband-to-be protested. "Well," she said, "you and your brother were spoiled rotten, for one thing." And on it went from there.

We eventually worked through this issue by having the couple agree to set limits (boundaries) as to gift giving by both sides of the family. Both parties agreed to support one another in setting boundaries with the future in-laws. The couple then asked their parents to also agree to those boundaries. This issue also has implications, which deal with *expectations* as discussed in Chapter IX, "Mind Games."

Establishing boundaries within family units is an important idea; however, to understand boundaries it is necessary first to understand how families function. Families are made up of various subsystems. For example, family subsystem divisions are made according to gender (male/female), generation (parents/children), common interests (intellectual/social), or function (who is responsible for what chores). These subsystems are defined by boundaries and rules for membership. Such boundaries determine who participates and what roles these participants will have in dealing with one another and with outsiders who are not part of the subsystem.

Clearly defined boundaries within the family unit and its various subsystems not only help maintain separateness, but also emphasize belonging to the same family system. Boundaries should be flexible enough so that care, support and involvement are available as needed.

Let me give an example of the way the establishment of such a boundary might work and how it might help to avoid conflict in a relationship: Newlyweds Bill and Susan were experiencing some in-law problems. Susan's parents lived nearby and frequently would drop in unannounced. In the beginning, both Bill and Susan enjoyed the visits, but over time they began to be a subject of contention. Bill's parents, on the other hand, never came around, but complained that since the wedding they hardly got to see Bill and Susan. Here is a case where the establishment of clear boundaries could eliminate problems for this young couple. First, they explained to Susan's parents that, while they loved seeing them, it was important their visits be scheduled to help Susan and Bill better regulate their time. Dropping in unannounced would therefore have to be curbed. Next, they met with Bill's parents and decided upon a visitation schedule. It was agreed, however, that this schedule would have to incorporate a degree of flexibility to accommodate Bill and Susan as well as Bill's parents.

Couples frequently have such boundary issues with parents or in-laws. Other issues (beside the ones just mentioned) might be: unwelcome financial support by parents or in-laws, spoiling grandchildren, or other child-raising issues, to name a few. These issues are best discussed (and agreed upon) so that proper boundaries can be set for the offending party. Parents and in-laws need to be informed of these boundaries. This is another aspect of good communication. For more information on this important subject, there is an excellent book entitled *Boundaries*, by Dr. Henry Cloud and Dr. John Townsend. Since many couples may not understand the concept of boundaries and their importance to a relationship, this book is highly recommended. Many of the problems experienced within families are boundary issues.

Perhaps then the most significant principle we can gain from this chapter is this:

> **PRINCIPLE:**
> Boundaries are important. Establishing boundaries early in a
> relationship will help minimize problems later on.

BIBLICAL COMMENTARY ON PARENTAL RELATION-SHIPS

Genesis 2:24 "For this reason a man will leave his father and mother and be united to his wife, and they will become one flesh."

This verse not only establishes God's intent for monogamous relationships, but also speaks of husband and wife leaving their previous family units and establishing an entirely new family unit, complete with its own priorities and its own new identity.

Exodus 20:12 "Honor your father and your mother, so that you may live long in the land the LORD your God is giving you."

This is the first commandment with a promise. Note, it does not say "honor your father and your mother if they are perfect," nor does it say "honor your father and mother if they are always right." This is a simple command to honor these two people who have brought you into this world. We honor them by listening to them and respecting their views—even though we may disagree with them. We honor them by helping to support them in their old age. At the very least, we honor them for giving us life.

Proverbs 10:1 "… A wise son brings joy to his father, but a foolish son grief to his mother."

Both this verse and the following one speak to the responsibility of children to bring honor and not dishonor to parents by making wise decisions rather than foolish ones.

Proverbs 13:24 "He who spares the rod hates his son, but he who loves him is careful to discipline him."

Parents who ignore discipline in the home are not rewarded with happy children. Children are always testing to see what the limits are, what exactly can they get away with. The parent who loves his children shows it by disciplining them. (Just as God disciplines those He loves.)

Proverbs 15:5 "A fool spurns his father's discipline, but whoever heeds correction shows prudence."

This verse deals with the child's response to discipline.

Proverbs 19:13 "A foolish son is his father's ruin …"

What we do reflects on our upbringing. This proverb also points out that others are affected by our actions.

Proverbs 23:22 "Listen to your father, who gave you life, and do not despise your mother when she is old."

This verse reinforces the command to honor our father and our mother.

Proverbs 29:15 "The rod of correction imparts wisdom, but a child left to himself disgraces his mother."

This verse is similar in tone to Proverbs 13:24 and deals with the importance and effects of discipline in the home.

Ephesians 6:4 "Fathers, do not exasperate your children; instead bring them up in the training and instruction of the Lord."

Just as the Bible instructs us to correct others with love, this verse speaks to the importance of being clear and loving and understanding with our children. We are to bring them up according to all that the Bible teaches about love, honor, and respect.

Hebrews 12:5–9 "... 'My son, do not make light of the Lord's discipline, and do not lose heart when he rebukes you, because the Lord disciplines those he loves, and he punishes everyone he accepts as a son. Endure hardship as discipline; God is treating you as sons. For what son is not disciplined by his father? If you are not disciplined (and everyone undergoes discipline), then you are illegitimate children and not true sons. Moreover, we have all had human fathers who disciplined us and we respected them for it. How much more should we submit to the Father of our spirits and live!"

This verse sums up many of the above verses. It points out not only that we discipline those we love in the same way God disciplines those He loves, but also, in the end, we respect those who discipline us.

Chapter XII

SEXUAL ASPECTS OF MARRIAGE

In this chapter, I have departed from the format of the previous chapters and have to a greater extent incorporated the biblical quotations into the text material. I have done this for two reasons. First, in the earlier chapters I have taken into account (and it is my desire) that many non-Christians would read this book and benefit from the secular as well as biblical wisdom contained herein. I therefore separated as much as possible the secular and the Christian thought (though, admittedly, at times this was impossible to do).

For example, the leading principle in this section is based solidly on biblical principle, yet supported solidly by secular statistics. The biblical wisdom that "marriage should be honored by all, and the marriage bed kept pure, for God will judge the adulterer and the sexually immoral" is backed up by the National Center for Health Statistics. Their research shows that if there has been regular sexual involvement before marriage the odds for divorce skyrocket. One obvious reason for this is that once couples become sexually intimate, their actions and decisions become clouded by emotions.

In this chapter, therefore, I felt that it would be difficult for me to separate biblical and secular wisdom. Secondly, I felt that the topic was such that all who had read to this point would read on.

Lust is such a strong emotion that the biblical admonition in matters of lust is always to flee from it. The Bible defines three types of sin: sins of the world, sins of the flesh, and sins of the devil. In each case the Bible outlines specific ways to fight those sins. In the case of sins of the flesh, we have numerous examples. For instance, in Genesis 39:12 we see Joseph confronted by Potiphar's wife: "She caught him by his cloak and said, 'Come to bed with me!' But he left his cloak in her hand and ran out of the house."

David, on the other hand, responded incorrectly, as we see in 2 Samuel 11:2, 4 where it says, "… he saw a woman bathing. The woman was very beautiful. Then David sent messengers to get her. She came to him, and he slept with her. …" Clearly when he first beheld this woman, instead of lingering and feeding his lust, he should have turned away and fled. Such is the power of lust, that fleeing from it is the only right course. This would be true when dealing with pornography as well. If on the Internet one were to encounter a pornographic site, immediately shutting it down is the only appropriate action. To linger is to sin and to be enticed to further viewing.

As with many of the chapters in this book, there is a degree of connectedness. While the subject of communication has been covered rather extensively in an earlier chapter, a few additional communication-related items should also be addressed here.

Often people avoid difficult or delicate subjects. Sex generally falls into one or both of these categories. In the book mentioned earlier (in the chapter on communication), *Christian Counseling* by Dr. Gary Collins, he says this: "If people cannot communicate in general, it is not likely they will be able to communicate about sex." He goes on to say, "Some people feel uncomfortable talking about sex, even with their own mates. To improve communication, encourage husbands and wives to share their feelings and attitudes about sex. Males do not automatically know how to stimulate a female and neither do all females know how to turn on a man. The husband and wife can tell each other what is stimulating. This communication should be honest, gentle and nonverbal as well as verbal. Taking the hand of one's mate and showing him or her how to stimulate can be an excellent communication technique."

Since we are not able to read each other's minds, it is imperative we communicate our wants, needs, and desires so we won't become frustrated by not being satisfied sexually. If we do not do so, our spouse will continue in ignorant bliss doing what he, or she, has always done. Learning to communicate more effectively in the sexual arena will go a long way toward improving our overall relationship and preventing future problems.

Sex is a very natural and necessary part of marriage. In the beginning, God stated our purpose on earth was to, "Be fruitful and increase in number" (Genesis 1:28). Humans were created to fill the earth and subdue it. God's plan was for the sexual act to be a part of the marriage arrangement. This is clear both in the above quotation from Genesis and from Genesis 2:24 where Scripture records these words, "For this reason man shall leave his father and mother and be united to his **wife**, and they will become one flesh" (emphasis added). The purpose for the sexual act is to populate the earth and reproduce our kind. This is made clear in the first verse given. The fact that sex was meant to be a part of the marriage relationship is made clear in the second verse.

Sex was designed for marriage. It should be kept for the marriage bed. With social diseases rampant, and no known cure for many of these diseases, it is more important now than ever before to save oneself for marriage. AIDS has added a further fatal dimension to this proclamation. These facts remain, regardless of religious beliefs. I know of no one who would intentionally bring a loved one some perilous and perhaps incurable disease or wish to risk acquiring one.

For example, when Mary found out from her doctor that her husband had given her an STD (sexually transmitted disease) she was furious. How could he have done this to her? She had never had sexual relations before marriage, and, although they had never specifically talked about it, she assumed they shared similar values.

I once saw a cartoon in which a grandson was discussing "safe sex" with his grandfather. The grandson said, "Grandpa, did they have condoms when you were young, or what did you use for protection?" The grandfather replied simply, "A wedding ring."

In 1 Corinthians 7:1–5, the Apostle Paul addresses the issue of sex and morality with these wise words: "… It is good for a man not to marry. But since there is so much immorality, each man should have his own wife, and each woman her own husband. The husband should fulfill his marital duty to his wife, and likewise the wife to her husband. The wife's body does not belong to her alone but also to her husband. In the same way, the husband's body does not belong to him alone but also to his wife. Do not deprive each other except by mutual consent and for a time, so that you may devote yourselves to prayer. Then come together again so that Satan will not tempt you because of your lack of self-control."

Couples should, whenever possible, agree to which sex acts are acceptable to them. If an act is offensive to one partner, it should be avoided out of respect for that partner. For couples previously married or who have already been sexually active, this discussion should take place beforehand to avoid a potential problem after the marriage has already been consummated. For those who have not been intimate before the marriage, these conversations should take place after sexual intimacy has been achieved. If a couple is already married and is having difficulties of this sort, a professional therapist should be consulted. These problems can usually be resolved to the satisfaction of both parties. The important thing is to discuss these matters openly and honestly and, when necessary, to seek professional help. (See also Chapter XIII, "Advice for Troubled Times.")

Dr. Collins, in *Christian Counseling*, also points out another key issue with regard to the sexual relationship, "Good sex, like good marriage, requires time, effort, and a willingness to work at making things better. If sex is to be satisfying and if serious sexual problems are to be prevented, a couple must always be alert to ways in which they can build a better relationship. This may involve reading about sex and trying new positions." He goes on to say, "Married people who get lax about personal hygiene, weight control, and physical appearance find that sex is less satisfying as they grow older."

The aspect of cleanliness, with regard to sexual relations, should not be minimized. Once, after a visit to Williamsburg, Virginia, and hearing about the appalling lack of dental and general hygiene practiced in Colonial times, my wife remarked that she was surprised our ancestors ever reproduced. This thought prompts me to re-emphasize the importance of always striving to keep clean and attractive for our spouse.

A further issue with regard to keeping ourselves physically attractive to our mate has to do with being physically fit. I have had spouses come to me complaining that their spouse had gained a great deal of weight, and this had resulted in the slimmer partner developing a "wandering eye." This is, of course, a worst-case scenario; a far more common reaction is the loss of interest in sexual relations. I must point out here that to blame a "wandering eye" on someone else is to attempt to shift blame for our actions to another person. Each of us is responsible for our own actions. No one has the power to make us act in an inappropriate way. Before marriage we must ask ourselves such hard questions as were asked in the first chapter of this book: "How would I react if my new spouse were suddenly rendered an invalid?" Or, "How would I react if my spouse put on a good deal of weight?" Life is not static. Changes occur, and often they are changes that are not favorable. Always remember, marriage is a lifetime commitment, a pledge before God, not something we should enter into without solemn thought and consideration.

It is worth noting here that sex for men is more in the nature of a physical urge. For a woman, it is a much more emotional act. A man, for instance, can be upset with his wife and yet still desire to have sexual relations. When a woman is upset with her husband, however, it is highly unlikely there will be any closeness in the marriage bed until some resolution is achieved. This is perhaps another reason for Paul's warning in his first letter to the Corinthians about the withholding of sexual favors within the marital framework.

Though sex should not be used as a weapon, it is imperative men realize how hard it is for a woman to separate it from her emotions. Love and sex are so closely associated that husbands must make every effort to make sure their wives feel loved. Words alone are not sufficient for a woman to feel loved; husbands must show them with actions just how precious they are. Husbands are called to love their wives "just as Christ loved the church" (see Ephesians 5:25). Since Christ died an agonizing death on the cross for the church, we can easily see this is a sacrificial and giving kind of love—an unconditional love.

What would we draw as a principle here that might serve to help "Beat the Marriage Odds"?

PRINCIPLE:
Sexual contact before marriage greatly lessens the odds for a successful marriage.

Note: If you are engaged or considering marriage and have already had sex with your partner, I recommend you cease doing so until after the wedding. I say this not for moral reasons alone or because it pleases God (though certainly these are most important factors). But, once two people begin having sexual relations, the whole issue of true love (love that can withstand hard times) becomes clouded with emotion; and it is key to remember love is not an emotion, it's a choice. Emotional marriages are the ones that most often end in divorce, so this is a key point!

BIBLICAL COMMENTARY ON SEXUAL RELATIONS

Genesis 1:28 "God blessed them and said to them, 'Be fruitful and increase in number ...'"

God's stated purpose for marriage here is clearly reproduction of the human race.

Genesis 2:20–25 "But for Adam no suitable helper was found. So the LORD God caused the man to fall into a deep sleep; and while he was sleeping, he took one of the man's ribs and closed up the place with flesh. Then the LORD God made a woman from the rib he had taken out of the man, and he brought her to the man. The man said, 'This is now bone of my bones and flesh of my flesh; she shall be called "woman" for she was taken out of man. For this reason a man will leave his father and mother and be united to his wife, and they will become one flesh.' The man and his wife were both naked, and they felt no shame."

The one flesh reference here is to the sexual union in the context of the monogamous, heterosexual relationship intended by God. Note also that the context of verse 25 is within the marital relationship.

1 Corinthians 7:1–5 "… It is good for a man not to marry. But since there is so much immorality, each man should have his own wife, and each woman her own husband. The husband should fulfill his marital duty to his wife, and likewise the wife to her husband. The wife's body does not belong to her alone but also to her husband. In the same way, the husband's body does not belong to him alone but also to his wife. Do not deprive each other except by mutual consent and for a time, so that you may devote yourselves to prayer. Then come together again so that Satan will not tempt you because of your lack of self-control."

Again the one-man-plus-one-woman aspect of marriage is brought out by the Apostle Paul as he here also addresses the issue of not withholding sexual favors from our spouse. Paul also points out the reason for this—that we not set ourselves up for temptation to sin.

Hebrews 13:4 "Marriage should be honored by all, and the marriage bed kept pure, for God will judge the adulterer and the sexually immoral."

This verse was covered in an earlier chapter and speaks to the sanctity of the marriage bed and the dangers presented by sex outside the context of marriage.

Chapter XIII

ADVICE FOR TROUBLED TIMES

In an ideal world we would all be perfect, act perfectly, and never need correction or redirection. Sadly, none of us meets those criteria. I see a simple answer to counseling. If we, as individuals, would take care of selfishness and pride, many counselors would be out of business. But, the reality is that, in the complex world of human emotions, simplistic answers seldom work. The following questions present themselves: "Why might we, as a couple, need help?" "Where might we go to get help?" and "When, or how soon, should we seek help?" This chapter answers those questions and also deals with some common misconceptions about counseling.

Outside assistance or counseling provides two essential elements for couples experiencing difficulties. First, a trained counselor can introduce new techniques and concepts to the troubled couple. Second, a counselor brings a fresh and objective viewpoint. Couples are usually too enmeshed in the problem to think or act objectively.

All too often, couples wait too long to go to a counselor for help. The sooner a problem is caught and corrected, the shorter the time usually required to fix the problem. I frequently find myself telling couples, "This problem didn't happen overnight, and, therefore, it probably won't be fixed overnight."

To illustrate how dangerous it can be to ignore problems, let's look at the following illustration: Dorothy and Bruce had been married for ten years. For all ten of those years, Dorothy had stuffed her feelings. Whenever she would try to explain how she felt, Bruce would glibly dismiss her concerns as silly or blame them on "her time of month." For ten years Dorothy tried to get Bruce to listen, to no avail. Then, one day Bruce came home from work and found a note. Dorothy had left him, stating simply that he never listened to her.

When marriage problems occur, seek help early. Don't wait until those problems become obscured by time and other complications. The longer problems simmer, the greater the complications that arise from them, and the more difficult they are to resolve. Often couples have waited so long they can't even remember when their troubles began, let alone the original cause. In such instances, their complaint is likely to sound something like, "We're just not compatible."

In an earlier chapter, I spoke briefly about abusive relationships. Destructive relationships are not always abusive relationships. Leslie Vernick has written a book entitled *The Emotionally Destructive Relationship: Seeing It, Stopping It, Surviving It*. She identifies five distinctive relationship patterns that are destructive: 1) physical, sexual, or emotional/verbal abuse; 2) a relationship characterized by one person being overprotective and/or overbearing; 3) a deceitful relationship involving hiding, lying, pretending, misleading, or twisting information to make someone or something other than what it is; 4) a relationship in which one person is overly dependent for their emotional, social, relational, spiritual, or economic needs to be met; 5) a pattern of indifference and/or neglect toward the thoughts, feelings, or well-being of the other in the relationship.

It is important for anyone suffering and in need of help to understand that the only person one can change is oneself. To say that we cannot change others is not the same as saying others cannot change. God is able to change or transform anyone. But it is important to recognize we are not God. Our best hope is to open our communication lines with Him. In that way, our prayers will be heard and our hope restored. And though it's always best to give things over to God, this is often difficult for us to do. Our human tendency is to take them back, or to never fully give them up at all.

I often use the illustration of the cross. When our eyes are focused on the horizontal (when we look at another person to satisfy or complete us or as the source of our troubles—a friend, spouse, employee/employer, etc.) we are bound for disappointment. It is only when we change our focus to the vertical (upward toward God) that relationships are restored. This is why Scripture records Jesus saying, "Anyone who loves his father or mother more than me is not worthy of me; anyone who loves his son or daughter more than me is not worthy of me" (Matthew 10:37). For some years I was troubled by this verse, until I came to the realization that unless I love Him as He intends I will never know how to love other people as I should. (To discover more about what the Bible says about how to live with a vertical view in mind, you may want to read Psalm 90.)

Those who are familiar with the Bible will recall that when Jesus called Simon Peter to step out of the boat to walk to Him on the water, Peter began to sink only after he looked away from Jesus. This is a tremendous picture of what happens when our upward gaze strays to the horizontal. We, too, begin to sink.

There is a popular therapy in use by many counselors today that is sometimes referred to as Solution-Focused Brief Therapy. Steven De Shazer developed his theories of Brief Therapy based in part on systems theory work by Milton Erickson. De Shazer contends that patients want to cooperate with the therapist, and it is the therapist's job to find a therapeutic approach that will quickly resolve the problem. The focus of this type of therapy is not on how problems arise, but on how to solve them. I have used this therapy successfully on a number of occasions.

What I like most about this type of therapy is that it offers some short-term relief and allows couples to see "light at the end of the tunnel."

An example of brief therapy follows: In a counseling session together, I asked both a husband and his wife to give me an example of something their spouse did (or didn't do) that particularly irritated them. The wife complained that, on many occasions, she would prepare dinner only to have her husband stop off after work for drinks at a bar with his friends. While waiting for her husband to come home, dinner would become cold, and the wife would become angry. The husband complained that his wife never wanted to have sex with him anymore. The couple never realized these two behaviors might, in some way, be related. The husband was mad at his wife because she had become frigid, so he stopped at the local hangout to commiserate with his friends. The wife was angry about her husband's failure to show up for dinner, and thus was not interested in physical relations with him.

To resolve this situation, I told the man (in his wife's presence) to make an effort the following week to come home for dinner on time without stopping by the pub—even suggesting he might bring his wife flowers. I asked the husband to record the days when he did this and to also record his wife's response. Likewise, I asked the wife (in the presence of her husband) to put on sexy lingerie several nights during the week and to plan a romantic evening for the two of them. I asked the wife to keep a record each time she did this, as well as her husband's subsequent response. The results were amazing to them, though not surprising to me. This was only a start in repairing the damage done over the years, but the results of using Brief Therapy gave the couple immediate hope and a renewed commitment to work together on their relationship. It also demonstrated to each the clear connection between positive actions and positive responses.

Brief Therapy can offer short-term relief for hurting couples. Often, the excuse couples use for not seeking counseling is they can't afford it. They envision a long, ongoing process. While there are times lengthy counseling must occur, it is usually because couples have waited too long before seeking counseling, or because they are slow or unwilling to accept the advice offered by the counselor. This can be a result of entrenched thinking, which has developed over time; thus even the recommendations of an objective third party are rejected or viewed with skepticism.

For other couples, the very idea of seeking professional help is a challenge that must be overcome before they can even begin the hard work of repairing their relationship. There are a number of reasons couples do not want to seek outside help. Often they believe they should be able to fix their problems themselves; or, as mentioned earlier, some couples think they cannot afford professional help; some suffer from the mistaken belief that "shrinks are for crazy people," and thus there is no application for their personal situation; or (as already mentioned) they may wait so long that it seems the problem can no longer be fixed.

In my opinion, none of the reasons listed above are valid reasons for failing to seek help. Let's take a look at each one of these objections couples might have in seeking professional help.

"I CAN FIX IT MYSELF." What most people embroiled in problems fail to realize is their thinking is usually impaired by the problem. You may have heard the line, "When you're up to your ears in alligators, it's hard to remember to drain the swamp!" Someone outside the situation can usually see alternatives that are not obvious to those who are too close to the problem. It is in these instances that clear objective thinking must be sought.

"WE CANNOT AFFORD PROFESSIONAL COUNSELING." Consider this: many churches offer professionally trained counselors. Some charge for this service, some do not. Still others offer the service on a pay-as-you can basis. Additionally, the American Association of Christian Counselors, a national organization that trains counselors, has a list of trained counselors who are available across the country. This information is available on their Web site, http://www.aacc.net/; by phone, 800-526-8673; by e-mail, CCC@AACC.net; or by mail, American Association of Christian Counselors, PO Box 739, Forest, VA 24551.

The AACC offers four different credentials. They are:

BCPCC—Board Certified Professional Christian Counselor— restricted to state-licensed mental health professionals with master's degrees or doctoral degrees who also practice as Christian counselors

BCCC—Board Certified Christian Counselor— for nonlicensed and pre-licensed Christian counselors who work and serve in a variety of helping and teaching roles

BCPC—Board Certified Pastoral Counselor— for ordained pastors and pastoral counselors engaged in significant counseling ministry in church and para-church settings

BCBC—Board Certified Biblical Counselor— for counselors with a bachelor's degree or counselors with associate degrees with some biblical and Christian counselor training and for advanced lay helpers with completed training.

Another organization, the National Association of Nouthetic Counselors, also trains counselors and publishes a list of counseling resources across the country. They may be contacted at National Association of Nouthetic Counselors, 5526 State Road 26 East, Lafayette, IN 47905; by phone, 765-448-9100; or e-mail, Info@NANC.org. Their Web site is www.nanc.org.

"SHRINKS ARE FOR CRAZY PEOPLE." At best, this is a misunderstanding of what marriage and family counseling is all about. Marriage and family counselors are often psychologists with doctorates. Sometimes they are merely counselors with a counseling certificate from an organization, like the two organizations mentioned above, who have received hours of either classroom or correspondence training. Often counselors are not psychiatrists (practitioners who have medical degrees and work with medical disorders that may require prescription medications).

Note: family issues sometimes involve a family member who is suffering with depression. Frequently these are not cases of clinical depression that would require medication. However, if the counselor determines an individual is clinically depressed, a referral would be made to someone qualified to further diagnose and treat, including prescribing medication. Also, there are occasions when a person may be suffering from bipolar disorder. This is sometimes misdiagnosed as depression. Bipolar disorder also would require treatment and prescription by a medical doctor.

"THE SITUATION SEEMS HOPELESS." This is the most common problem I encounter. In these situations, I frequently hear husbands saying, "You must talk to my wife!" Or I hear from wives who say, "You've got to talk to my husband." My response, in most cases, is: *"You're here.* Tell me what's going on." It is not the therapist's job to solicit individuals to come in for counseling.

I highly recommend a wonderful book by Michele Weiner-Davis, entitled *Divorce Busting: A Step-by-Step Approach to Making Your Marriage Loving Again.* This is an excellent resource for anyone whose family situation has deteriorated to a seemingly hopeless state. This book has a chapter entitled, "It Takes One to Tango: Change Your Marriage by Changing Yourself." In this chapter, the author makes the statement: "Your spouse doesn't have to read this book in order for the methods to be effective. In fact, your spouse doesn't even have to overtly agree to wanting to make the marriage work." This book is also based on Solution-Oriented Brief Therapy or Quick Therapy, which I referenced earlier in this chapter. Her Web site, http://www.divorcebusting.com/, also offers many helpful resources.

After working with one marriage partner, helping him (or her) to make changes and be more positive about himself (or herself), and to recognize the roles that he (or she) played in the relationship problems, I have at times had the other spouse come to counseling and comment, "I've noticed such a change in my husband/wife. What have you been doing?" Or simply, "Do you think you can help us?" My advice is usually, "Don't wait! It's easier to fix issues now than it will be next month or next year."

Many local priests, pastors, and rabbis offer counseling. The quality of that counseling will vary greatly depending on both individual skills and training. Often pastors with a master of divinity degree have had only a basic three-hour basic course in counseling. This is generally not sufficient to deal with many of the problems couples face today. However, many pastors have had additional training and are quite gifted. I always recommend asking about the professional training and educational background of a counselor. I also recommend that when both parties agree to counseling, they both be comfortable with the counselor. Additionally, both should agree to be open to the recommendations of that counselor. In instances where one of the parties does not like or respect the counselor, no positive change is likely to occur.

Here is the principle I consider most important for couples to take away from this chapter.

> **PRINCIPLE:**
> **In a troubled relationship, seek qualified private or professional help early!**

BIBLICAL VERSES ABOUT TROUBLED TIMES

I Kings 22:5 "But Jehoshaphat also said to the king of Israel, 'First seek the counsel of the LORD.'"

God's counsel, which should rightly be our first resource, is all too often the one we turn to last—when all else has failed. This same thing is frequently the case with human counsel. Couples often wait too long before seeking help in their troubled relationships.

Psalm 73:23–24 "Yet I am always with you; you hold me by my right hand. You guide me with your counsel ..."

God is always there for us. Unmoving. Unchangeable. He waits patiently for us to seek His help.

Proverbs 15:22 "Plans fail for lack of counsel, but with many advisers they succeed."

This verse points to the wisdom of Solomon. Seek outside, objective help whenever possible. The wisdom of many is usually better than the wisdom of one.

John 14:16-17 "And I will ask the Father, and he will give you another Counselor to be with you forever—the Spirit of truth. …"

Many see this as one of the greatest promises of Scripture. God has given us the Holy Spirit, Who is always there for us. The only question: Are we listening?

Chapter XIV

USEFUL FORMS FOR PREMARITAL COUNSELING

1) **Wedding Planner** This handy form lists key information, such as names, dates, places, contacts, etc.

2) **Suggested Outline for Counseling** These counseling sessions can be adjusted to suit the schedules of those involved. This is only one of a number of possible counseling scenarios (complete with homework and reading assignments). It has been my experience that if couples are unwilling to put time and effort into a relationship before marriage, they are unlikely to do so after marriage.

3) **Family History** This is a guide to the kinds of information that will be helpful in assessing future areas of potential concern in a relationship, i.e. health (both mental and physical) and safety (patterns of abuse) issues, and possible relational problems (sibling rivalries, enmeshed families, etc.).

WEDDING PLANNER

Bride'sName:_____

               First   *M.I.*   *Last*

Phone:_____

Bride's Parents:

Mother: _____

Father:_____

Groom'sName:_____

               First   *M.I.*   *Last*

Phone: _____

Groom's Parents:

Mother: _____

Father: _____

Rehearsal dinner:

At: _____

Day: _____ Time: _____

Date of Wedding: _____

Time of Wedding: _____

Place of Wedding: _____

Place of Reception: _____

Time of Reception: _____

Maid/Matron of Honor: _____

Best Man: _____

Bridesmaids: _____

_____

_____

_____

_____

Groomsmen: _____

_____

_____

_____

_____

Personal touches (Soloist, Unity Candle, Personalized Vows,

Special Readings, etc.)

_____

_____

_____

_____

_____

_____

_____

SUGGESTED OUTLINE FOR COUNSELLING

SESSION I (approximately two hours*)

A)   An overview of what will be covered and best times to meet.

B) Have the couple fill out marriage planner. This will provide all of the names, dates, times, locations, contact information, and other essential information for their file.

C) Watch the film *I Do: Portraits From Our Journey*, available through the Family Research Council.

D) Review the film and the accompanying workbook.

E) Homework Assignment: Read Genesis 1:26–28; Genesis 2:24; Genesis 3; 1 Corinthians chapters 7 and 13. Read the book *The Five Love Languages: How to Express Heartfelt Commitment to Your Mate* by Dr. Gary Chapman. Read the first five chapters of *Beating the Marriage Odds*.

SESSION II (approximately two hours*)

A)   Definition of Marriage:
  - Your view
  - Popular worldview
  - Biblical view

B)   Discuss what it means to have a Christ-centered marriage.

C)   Definition of Love:
  - Your view
  - Popular worldview
  - Biblical view

D)   Review couples' love languages, and talk about the importance of fulfilling your partner's needs.

E)   Homework: Read the book *Love and Respect* and read chapters VI and VII of *Beating the Marriage Odds*.

SESSION III (approximately two hours*)

A)   Discuss communication.

B)   Discuss finances.

C)   Discuss aspects of how to argue without hurting your relationship.

D)   Homework: Read Chapters IX through XIII of *Beating the Marriage Odds*. Fill out family history forms. Optional—*Read How to Manage Your Money* by Dr. Larry Burkett.

SESSION IV (approximately two hours*)

A)   Discuss "Mind Games" (expectations, assumptions, assigning motives, and mind reading).

B)   Review family histories and discuss potential problem areas.

C)   Discuss family relationships: parents, in-laws, siblings, etc.

D)   Discuss sexual aspects of marriage.

E)   Discuss the "when and where" of seeking outside help.

F)   Discuss any follow-up counseling, if and when required.

*Note: Times usually need to be adjusted to accommodate the schedules of the couple. Instead of four two-hour sessions, you may do eight one-hour sessions, three three-hour sessions, or even, at times, one all-day session (although such a session is less desirable as it does not allow for homework assignments and adequate information gathering). If an all-day session becomes necessary, I recommend (whenever possible) assigning all reading and homework well in advance.

FAMILY HISTORY

For Bride's Side and Groom's Side

• List relatives, living and deceased, on both father's and mother's sides, going back at least to grandparents—father, mother, aunts, uncles, siblings.

• List important details about each person, especially problems related to drug, alcohol, physical, verbal, or sexual abuse; suicides; or any history of mental illness.

• If deceased, state age at death and cause of death (list pertinent health history, such as mental problems, diabetes, cancer, heart disease, or other issues).

• If not an only child, list your place in the birth order (i.e. firstborn, middle child, last child, etc.).

• List any other facts you consider important, such as divorce and/ or remarriage of any family members. Also mention any relationships that are especially close or distant, etc.

Bride's Family

Grandparents	Paternal	Maternal
Living or dead	☐	☐
If dead, age at death	☐	☐
Married or Divorced	☐	☐
Any history of abuse?	☐	☐
Key health issues	☐	☐

	Father	Mother
Living or dead	☐	☐
If dead, age at death	☐	☐
Married or Divorced	☐	☐
Any history of abuse?	☐	☐
Key health issues	☐	☐

Brothers/Sisters

Number of each _____

Age of each _____

Your birth order, i.e., First/middle/Last_____

Married/Divorced _____

Relationship, i.e., (good, bad, strained) _____

Bride Groom

Previously married, Yes or No: _____

If yes, children by previous marriage, Yes or No: _____

Boys_____ Girls _____

Ages_____

Reason(s) for divorce: _____

_____

_____

Ex living locally , Yes or No: _____

Custody of children, Yes or No: _____

Groom's Family

Grandparents	Paternal	Maternal
Living or dead	☐	☐
If dead, age at death	☐	☐
Married or Divorced	☐	☐
Any history of abuse?	☐	☐
Key health issues	☐	☐

	Father	Mother
Living or dead	☐	☐
If dead, age at death	☐	☐
Married or Divorced	☐	☐
Any history of abuse?	☐	☐
Key health issues	☐	☐

Brothers/Sisters

Number of each _____

Age of each _____

Your birth order, i.e., First/middle/Last_____

Married/Divorced _____

Relationship, i.e., (good, bad, strained) _____

Bride Groom

Previously married, Yes or No: _____

If yes, children by previous marriage, Yes or No: _____

Boys_____ Girls _____

Ages_____

Reason(s) for divorce: _____

_____

_____

Ex living locally , Yes or No: _____

Custody of children, Yes or No: _____

Chapter XV

SAMPLE WEDDING CEREMONIES
Plus PASTORAL TIPS

This chapter includes the following:

1)   A ceremony acknowledging God

2)   A Christian ceremony, acknowledging both God and Christ

3)   A 2nd Christian ceremony, appropriate where both families have strong Christian traditions

4)   A 3rd Christian ceremony, appropriate for families of mixed beliefs and for couples who may have accepted Christ during counseling, or rededicated their lives to Christ

5)   Pastoral tips

Some of the ceremonies presented here were excerpted from the book *Tools for the Shepherd* by Steve Dahrens.

A Wedding Ceremony

(Acknowledging God)

We are gathered together here in the presence of God to join _____ and _____ in holy matrimony, which has been instituted by God and regulated by His commandments. Marriage is a joyous occasion. It is connected in our thoughts with the charm of home, and with all that is pleasant and attractive in all the most sacred relations of life. God has instructed those who enter into this relationship to cherish a mutual esteem and love; to bear with each others weaknesses and infirmities, to comfort one another in sickness, trouble, and sorrow; in honesty and industry to provide for each other, and to live together as heirs to the grace of life.

Will you bow with me now for a moment of prayer?

God, we thank You for this beautiful day that You have given us for this wonderful occasion. We pray that this marriage, which is about to be performed, would be blessed by You, and that You would be an ever-present blessing to this relationship. Amen.

Song (optional)

Who gives _____ (*bride*) to be married to _____ (*groom*)? (*Father or both parents of bride respond and sit down.*)

One of the best descriptions of love ever written records these words from 1 Corinthians 13: "Love is patient, love is kind. It does not envy, it does not boast, it is not proud. It is not rude, it is not self-seeking, it is not easily angered, it keeps no record of wrongs. Love does not delight in evil but rejoices with the truth. It always protects, always trusts, always hopes, always perseveres. Love never fails. ... Now these three remain: faith, hope and love, but the greatest of these is love."

_____ and _____ have come here today to make public their love for one another, and to declare their choice to live, to partner, and to grow together in the bond of matrimony. It is their desire that all who are present here today might also take this opportunity to rededicate their own bonds of love.

Both _____ and _____ see marriage as "opportunities" rather than as "obligations"—opportunities for growth and for the realization of all that God has for them.

If this, _____ (groom), is an expression of your desires, say, "It is."

Groom responds.

And, _____ (bride), if this also is an expression of your desires, say, "It is."

Bride responds.

You will find, _____ (*groom*), that because _____ (*bride*) gives her life, her love, her self—all that she is and ever can be—to you, this is the finest gift that can come to you as a man. Your responsibility is to be for her sake the truest and finest man you can be, to be worthy of her love.

And you, _____ (*bride*), will find the same, because _____ (*groom*) gives you his name, his honor, his life, his love, himself—all that he is and ever can be—to you, to be yours alone forever. This is the tremendous crowning gift fit for your womanhood, and your responsibility is to be to him the finest partner in the world.

Pick up roses.

As a symbol of their love, one for the other, _____ and _____ have chosen the rose. I now give you these two red roses. Please exchange these roses as an indication of your understanding of this new relationship you are about to enter into and a symbol of your love, one for the other.

Now, please take this white rose. White stands for God's purity. Let this remind you of God's deep love for you both. With the three roses we begin to form a picture of God's intended marital plans for man. Picture a triangle. At the lower two corners are two red roses, representing husband and wife. At the apex is a single white rose, representing God. As the couple grows closer to the apex (draws nearer to God), they also grow closer to each other. This is what intended by the Scripture recorded in Ecclesiastes 4:9–12, which says: "Two are better than one, because they have a better return for their work: If one falls down, his friend can help him up. … Also, if two lie down together, they will keep warm. But how can one keep warm alone? Though one may be overpowered, two can defend themselves. A cord of three strands is not quickly broken."

Song (optional)

What additional symbols do you bring of the promises given and received here today?

Groom answers: "Wedding rings."

These rings are a reminder of life as God intended—a life with no beginning and no end. They are a symbol of completeness—just as each of you is meant to complete the other.

(*To groom*) Do you, _____, have a token of this covenant?

Please repeat after me: I, _____ (*groom*), give you, _____ (bride), this ring as a pledge and a token of my constant faith and abiding love.

(*To bride*) Do you, _____ , have a token of this covenant?"

Please repeat after me: I, _____ (*bride*), give you, _____ (groom), this ring as a pledge and a token of my constant faith and abiding love.

Forasmuch as you, _____ (*groom*), and you, _____ (*bride*), have consented together in holy marriage, and have witnessed the same before God and this company, by the authority committed unto me as a minister of Jesus Christ, according to the ordinance of God and the laws of the State of _____, I now pronounce you husband and wife.

You may kiss the bride.

I now have the honor of presenting to you Mr. And Mrs. _____ _____ .

A Christian Wedding

(Acknowledging both God and Christ)

We are gathered here in the presence of God to unite this man and this woman by the sacred ties of marriage. (May use the names of the bride and groom in place of "man" and "woman.")

Who gives _____ (*bride*) to be married to _____ (*groom*)? (*Father or both parents of bride respond and sit down.*)

Let us come together before our great God and Savior for His blessings on this precious event. *Offer prayer.*

Those who take the holy vows of marriage are brought into the closest and most sacred of all human relationships. These two lives will be blended into one to share the great joys and trials of life. From this close, intimate relationship spring obligations of the most solemn and lasting character. The husband is under obligation to protect his wife, to love her in the same way Christ loved the church, which is a sacrificial and giving love. And the wife is under an obligation to respect her husband and to submit to him as to the Lord.

145

Both should offer the kind of love the Apostle Paul described to the Corinthians. *Here read 1 Corinthians 13 from The Message*: "If I speak with human eloquence and angelic ecstasy but don't love, I'm nothing but the creaking of a rusty gate. If I speak God's Word with power, revealing all mysteries and making everything plain as day, and if I have a faith that says to a mountain, 'Jump,' and it jumps, but I don't love, I'm nothing. If I give everything I own to the poor and even go the stake to be burned as a martyr, but I don't love, I've gotten nowhere. So, no matter what I say, what I believe, and what I do, I'm bankrupt without love. Love never gives up. Love cares more for others than for self. Love doesn't want what it doesn't have. Love doesn't strut, Doesn't have a swelled head, Doesn't force itself on others, Isn't always "me first," Doesn't fly off the handle, Doesn't keep score of the sins of others, Doesn't revel when others grovel, Takes pleasure in the flowering of truth, Puts up with anything, Trusts God always, Always looks for the best, Never looks back, But keeps going to the end. But for right now, … we have three things … Trust steadily in God, hope unswervingly, love extravagantly. And the best of the three is love."

Will You, _____ (*groom*), have this woman whose hand you hold, to be your wedded wife, and solemnly promise that you will loyally fulfill your obligation as her husband to love her, protect her, honor her, and cherish her in adversity as well as prosperity, and to keep yourself unto her alone, so long as you both shall live? If so, answer, "I will."

Groom responds.

And will you, _____ (*bride*), have this man whose hand you hold, to be your wedded husband, and solemnly promise that you will be unto him a tender, respectful, and true wife through sunshine and shadow alike, and be faithful to him so long as you both shall live? If so, answer, "I will."

Bride responds.

(*Prayer*) God, at this time we ask that You would look with loving favor upon this couple as they make their vows before you. We thank you for your providence, which has brought them together here today, and we pray this would not be an outer act only, made with human words, but that it would truly be a commitment of will before a holy God; an inner blending of heart, spirit, and purpose. Establish in them qualities that make a good marriage: loyalty, honor, purity, self-control, trust, forgiveness, and cooperation. Lord, we praise You for what You will do in their lives, for You are the master of the art of living.

What tokens do you have as a reminder of this day before God?

Groom answers: "Wedding rings."

This ring has a great significance, and holds many symbolic truths. Gold, most precious among metals, represents the precious ties that unite a husband and wife. Being round in shape, these rings have no beginning and no end. They symbolize the unbroken partnership between husband and wife, "'til death do you part," and should be constant reminders to you both of the commitment you have made to one another before God this day.

(*Groom*) As you put this ring on your bride's finger, repeat after me: "I, _____, give this ring to you, _____, and declare by this act, in the presence of God and this company, that I take you to be my wedded wife, and that I shall be faithful to you until death shall part us."

(*Bride*) As you place this ring on your groom's finger, repeat after me: "I, _____, give this ring to you, _____, and declare by this act, in the presence of God and this company, that you are the husband of my choice, and that I will be faithful to you until death shall part us."

The minister shall now say, "As you go forth in this new relationship, you will face new challenges, new situations, and greater responsibilities. I charge you both to be true to these vows you have made this day, before God and these witnesses. Trust God in all things. Strive daily to become more Christlike, and as you both grow in the image of Christ, you will find that you will naturally both draw closer, one to the other."

For as much as you, _____, and you, _____, have open-ly declared your wishes to be united in marriage, and in the presence of God and this company have pledged love and fidelity to each other, and having confirmed the same by giving a ring and joining hands, I, as a minister of Christ's Church, and legally authorized by the State of _____, do now pronounce you husband and wife.

You may kiss the bride.

I now present to you Mr. And Mrs. _____ _____.

A Second Christian Wedding Ceremony

(Both from Christian families)

Seat the audience.

We have come together today to be a part of one of the most sacred and exciting events that can take place on earth. We have the opportu-nity to witness here today two people being joined in holy matrimony.
We believe that God has led _____ and _____ to come into the same path. Since I have met these two, I have had the joy of observing many things, among them: (*List some below*)

1.
2.
3.

Let us pray for this union together. Dear God, it is You who first sanctioned marriage and gave it purpose. As we stand before You today, we ask that You bless this union between _____ and _____. We pray especially that the vows they are about to exchange would be honoring to You, and acknowledged by them as holy and sacred. Bless us this day, in the name of your Son, Jesus Christ. Amen.

Who gives this woman to be married to this man?

[*Or*: Who gives _____ (*bride*) to be married to _____ (*groom*)?] (*Father or both parents of bride respond and sit down.*)

Song or Special Music here, if desired

If couple desires to share a significant Scripture or two:
* *Chapter and verse*
* *Chapter and verse*

Pastor summarizes the significance of what is shared.

(*Groom*) _____, if you continue to grow in the Lord and continue to call upon Him, He will make _____ (*bride*) always as desirable and beautiful as you see her today. Continue to meet daily at the feet of the Savior, and He will grant His personal blessing on this union. Daily ask the Lord to bless _____ (*bride*), and you will yourself be blessed.

(*Bride*) _____ , what a privilege to find a man such as _____ (*groom*), who loves the Lord as he does. _____ (*groom*) will be held accountable before the Lord for the success of this marriage and the family to come. He gives himself to you with joy; he gives you his name, most precious to him, that you might be his own forever. You are to encourage him in the Lord.

I challenge you both to lift up and encourage one another daily. I likewise challenge you to esteem one another as best friends, most precious to each other, and to always pray together each day.

VOWS (*May also be memorized and recited.*)

If memorized: _____, would you share your promise with the Lord today?

Or, repeat after me:

(*Groom*) I, _____, take you, _____, to be my wedded wife, to have and to hold from this day forward. For better or for worse, for richer for poorer, in sickness and in health, to love and to cherish, to lead and to provide, forsaking all others, until death itself parts us, according to God's Holy ordinance; I therefore pledge you my life as a loving and faithful husband.

(*Bride*) I, _____, take you, _____, to be my wedded husband, to have and to hold from this day forward. For better or for worse, for richer for poorer, in sickness and in health, to love and to cherish, to respect and to obey, forsaking all others until death itself parts us, according to God's holy ordinance; I therefore pledge to you my life as a loving and faithful wife.

RING CEREMONY

(*Groom*) _____, what will you give today to cause you to remember these vows before God?

Groom answers: "A ring."

The ring is a fitting symbol for this remembrance. Gold is most precious among metals, and symbolizes the precious ties that unite husband and wife. It is round in shape and has no beginning and no end—it is endless, symbolizing an unbroken partnership until death. The ring should be a constant reminder of your commitment to each other.

(*Groom*) _____, as you place this ring on _____'s finger, recite after me: "I, _____, give you this ring as a pledge and a token of my constant faith and abiding love."

(*Bride*) _____, as you place this ring on _____'s finger recite after me: "I, _____, give you this ring as a pledge and a token of my constant faith and abiding love."

SPECIAL MUSIC AND/OR LIGHTING OF UNITY CANDLE (OPTIONAL)

(Also, roses may be presented to parents during the song if desired.)

_____ and _____ , because you have consented together in holy marriage before Almighty God and this company, by the authority given to me by the laws of God as a minister of Christ's Church and the State of _____, I now pronounce you husband and wife.

You may kiss the bride.

I now present the new Mr. And Mrs. _____ _____.

Encourage family and friends to support the new couple. Example: I would encourage you, as family and friends, to strongly support this couple. In this day and age, and with an increasingly high rate of divorce, couples are often encouraged to give up. It's easy to take sides in a time of conflict, but always encourage them to stay together; don't let them quit. Remind them of the vows they've made here today. "For better or for worse, in sickness and in health, to love and to cherish, until death parts them." Remember, this is not a marriage contract; it is a covenant before God. Good friends give good advice. Use godly counsel, not human wisdom. I encourage you to stand behind them, support them, and make this marriage God honoring. God Bless!

A Third Christian Wedding
(For Christian families and for those couples who have accepted Christ during counseling or rededicated their lives)

Seat the audience.

We are gathered together here in the presence of God to join _____ (*groom*) and _____ (*bride*) in holy marriage, which has been instituted by God and regulated by His commandments. Marriage is a joyous occasion. It is connected in our thoughts with the charm of home and with all that is pleasant and attractive in the tenderest and most sacred relations of life. A wedding in Cana of Galilee was sanctioned and cheered by the presence of the Lord Jesus Himself; and marriage is declared by an inspired apostle to be honorable. God has instructed those who enter into this relationship to cherish a mutual esteem and love; to bear with each other's infirmities and weaknesses; to comfort one another in sickness, trouble, and sorrow; in honesty and industry to provide for each other and in the things that pertain to God; and to live together as heirs to the grace of God.

Please pray with me. Dear God, we thank You for this day You have provided for this blessed event. We pray for Your presence in this new relationship, that You would bless it, be a central part of it, and guide the path of these two as they enter into a new chapter in their lives. Amen.

Who gives this woman to be married to this man?
(*Father or parents of bride respond and sit down.*)

We are indeed happy both of you have taken Jesus Christ as your Savior and Lord, according to His purpose, and that He has brought you together to be a further testimony to Himself.

You are now entering a new sphere of life, and we desire to have you place God first in all your plans; consult Him is every action; seek Him in every trial; trust Him in every moment; live in the light of His presence; and meet daily together at the throne of His grace.

You will find, _____ (*groom*), that because _____ (*bride*) has given her life, her love, her self—all that she is and ever can be—to be yours, and yours alone forever, this is the finest gift that can come to you as a man. And your responsibility is to be for her sake the truest and finest man you can be, to be worthy of her love.

And you, _____ (*bride*), will find the same, because _____ (*groom*) gives you his name, his life, his love, himself—all that he is and can be—to be yours and yours alone forever; this is the tremendous crowning gift fit for your womanhood. And your responsibility is to be to him the finest partner in the world.

I charge you both, therefore, to mean everything in the world to each other, for the sake of your happiness in Jesus Christ, the Lord.

(*Groom*) _____, do you take this woman to be your wedded wife, to live together after God's ordinance in the holy estate of marriage? Do you pledge to love her, comfort her, honor her, and keep her in sickness and in health, and, forsaking all others, cleave only unto her, so long as you both shall live?

Groom answers, "I do."

(*Bride*) _____, do you take this man to be you wedded husband, to live together after God's ordinance in the holy estate of marriage? Do you pledge to love him, comfort him, honor him, and keep him in sickness and in health, and, forsaking all others, cleave only unto him, so long as you both shall live?

Bride answers, "I do."

VOWS (*Couple may join hands*)

Repeat after me:

I, _____ (*groom*), take you, _____ (*bride*), to be my wedded wife, to have and to hold from this day forward, for better or worse, for richer for poorer, in sickness or in health, to love and to cherish, 'til death do us part, according to God's holy ordinance; and thereto I pledge you my love.

I, _____ (*bride*), take you, _____ (*groom*), to be my wedded husband, to have and to hold from this day forward, for better or worse, for richer for poorer, in sickness or in health, to love honor and obey, 'til death do us part, according to God's holy ordinance; and thereto I pledge you my love.

SPECIAL MUSIC OR A UNITY CANDLE MAY BE IN-TRODUCED

RING CEREMONY

Do you have a token of this covenant?

The groom (or both) shall say, "I do."

The minister shall then say, "Repeat after me: I, _____ (*groom*), give you, _____ (*bride*), this ring as a pledge and a token of my constant faith and abiding love."

The bride shall then repeat: "I, _____, give you, _____ (*groom*), this ring as a pledge and a token of my constant faith and abiding love."

Will you pray with me? Dear God, we thank You for Your plan of marriage. We ask that You would bless this union here today. That You would be present at all times in this marriage, that You would encourage them and strengthen them, and we ask that You grant them wisdom.

For as much as you, _____ (*groom*), and you, _____ (*bride*), have consented together in holy marriage and have witnessed the same before God and this company, by the authority committed unto me as a minister of Jesus Christ, according to the ordinance of God and the laws of the State of _____, I now pronounce you husband and wife.

You may kiss the bride.

I now present the new Mr. And Mrs. _____ _____.

PASTORAL TIPS

Whenever possible, my wife and I do marital and premarital counseling as a team. If you are married, I would suggest your wife participate whenever possible. This has a number of distinct advantages: 1) Women have entirely different perspectives on many issues and can communicate different viewpoints; 2) Women often are more intuitive than men and pick up on issues that might otherwise be overlooked; and 3) Couples being counseled are able to observe a model of healthy interaction between a husband and a wife and are often able to observe healthy ways to disagree. (Yes, my wife and I do disagree on some issues.) Disagreements are a part of life, a part of marriage, and learning to deal with them in healthy and productive ways is perhaps the most important aspect of developing a healthy relationship.

Premarital counseling is only as effective as we make it. The depth and breadth of the materials covered has a great impact on just how effective your counseling is. My wife and I often find couples coming to us who have had other counseling. The most oft-heard complaint is that a counselor never mentioned anything about a particular subject, such as expectations. Never having anticipated a particular problem simply leads couples into uncharted waters. Obviously, we cannot cover every eventuality, but the greater the amount of scenarios we can cover, the greater the odds of success.

Often a counselor has failed to consider disparate backgrounds, and problems have arisen because of huge gaps in interest or upbringing. The more in-depth the counseling, the greater the odds the couple will be able to recognize and deal with issues as they arise. Perhaps the greatest service we can provide as counselors is to help them to expect rough spots in their relationship and to encourage them to seek help early. Generally, the longer a problem or bad habit exists, the longer the time required to fix the problem; and lengthy times of trial lead to frustration, which in turn leads to anger, and can eventually place couples in an endless cycle of disagreement.

A PERSONAL NOTE:

This book is only a guide. It can be added to or subtracted from to suit individual needs. It is provided as a starting point. If you have subjects you normally cover in counseling that are not included here, I would be most interested in your input. We are always interested in helping couples to better deal with their relationships, to anticipate problems, and to handle them in more constructive ways.

You may e-mail me at marriage@blackfoot.net or write to William R. Campbell, P.O. Box 914, Seeley Lake, MT 59868. Or visit the www. BeatingtheMarriageOdds.com web site.

EPILOGUE
To the Couple

You may recall that at the beginning of this book I asked you to define what it means to be a Christian and what God requires of us to be saved. Later, I asked you if you would like to make a decision for Christ. I again cautioned that becoming a Christian is not a decision to make lightly (either to please your pastor, a relative, or for some other unworthy reason). A decision to follow Christ must be a decision of both your heart and your mind—a confession of your mouth that "Jesus is Lord" and a belief in your heart that God raised Him from the dead. Your individual decisions will determine the type of marriage ceremony and the words spoken at your ceremony.

Some of the principles outlined in this book may not apply to your relationship; others certainly will. Some principles will have a greater potential for impact on your marriage than others. I have seen the results of these principles in action. I can assure you that if you studiously and regularly employ them, they will strengthen and improve your marital relationship. You will find in marriage, as in most other areas of your life, that you will reap in accordance with what you sow.

Marriage, however, involves two people. And since a person can only control one-half of the marriage equation, a particular outcome is never assured. God only holds us responsible for our own individual actions—never for the actions of another. In his book *Quiet Strength: The Principles, Practices, & Priorities of a Winning Life*, Tony Dungy points out that fifty percent of failed NFL marriages occur in the first year after retirement. Every profession is fraught with its own set of stresses and pressures. Yet, though there are many causes for divorce, the principles contained in this book—when applied—will help beat the marriage odds.

Nothing is more satisfying to me than to complete a day in the sure knowledge I have done my very best. Even though I may fall short in an area or two, I am happy if I can simply say, "Today was a little better than yesterday. Tomorrow will be better still." If I do my part, I know God will always do His, for He is ever faithful. Growth is an ongoing process. Since we are all creatures of habit, and since those habits are both bad and good, we must constantly strive to replace bad habits with good ones. This book is actually a list of habits, which have proved useful in mending, repairing, and strengthening marriage relationships. My wife and I pray that you will use them to strengthen and improve your own marriage relationship.

REVIEW OF PRINCIPLES

CHAPTER I

Things to Consider Before You Say, "'Til Death Do Us Part!"

PRINCIPLE:

Consider, and take to heart, every aspect of the marriage vows before making a "'til death do us part" solemn promise to God and to your spouse.

CHAPTER II

The Marriage Myth

PRINCIPLES:

For couples who believe in God, a three-way covenant relationship offers greater strength than a mere two-way contractual relationship.

The closer you come to putting 100 percent effort into your marriage, the greater your odds are for a successful marriage.

CHAPTER III

The "D" word

PRINCIPLE:

Enter your marriage with the mutual understanding that divorce will not be discussed in your home, nor will it be an option for you (not a change *of* partners, but a change *in* the partners).

CHAPTER IV

True Love

PRINCIPLES:

The greater our will or determination for a successful marriage, the greater our odds are for the reality of a successful marriage.

Being equally yoked, or compatible, greatly increases the odds for a successful marriage.

CHAPTER V
Trust—The Foundation for a Lasting Relationship
PRINCIPLE:
In a marriage, your word is quite literally your bond. To destroy that bond is to undermine the very foundation of the marriage!

CHAPTER VI
Communication—The Leading Cause of Marital Breakdowns
PRINCIPLE:
Studying and improving your communication skills will pay immediate dividends to all of your personal relationships!

CHAPTER VII
Finances—The Second Leading Cause of Marital Breakdowns
PRINCIPLE:
A focus on sound financial practices, such as controlling spending (needs vs. wants) and limiting debt (tear up credit cards—if you don't have the money, you can't afford it!) will pay huge dividends for every relationship.

CHAPTER VIII
Fight Fair—The Upside of Arguments
PRINCIPLE:
Be alert to the following symptoms of a deteriorating relationship: 1) criticism of your spouse as a person rather than criticism of behavior; 2) showing contempt for your spouse; 3) becoming defensive in your relationship, and 4) stonewalling or refusal to interact with your spouse. Recognize the symptoms, and immediately take steps to correct them!

CHAPTER IX
Mind Games—Expectations, Assumptions, Assigning Motives, and Other Dangerous Games

PRINCIPLE:

Avoidance of unrealistic expectations, assumptions, sweeping generalities, and jumping to conclusions will enhance all of your personal relationships.

CHAPTER X
Assigning Roles
PRINCIPLE:

Marriage is a team sport; develop a team mentality and work ethic in your home.

CHAPTER XI
In-Laws/Out-Laws
PRINCIPLE:

Boundaries are important. Establishing boundaries early in a relationship will minimize problems later on.

CHAPTER XII
Sexual Aspects of Marriage
PRINCIPLE:

Sexual contact before marriage greatly lessens the odds for a successful marriage.

CHAPTER XIII
Advice for Troubled Times
PRINCIPLE:

In a troubled relationship, seek qualified private or professional help early!

REVIEW QUESTIONS BY CHAPTER

CHAPTER I

1. What is the most important point you took from this chapter?

_____

_____

_____

_____

_____

2. What is your understanding of the word "vow"?

_____

_____

_____

_____

_____

3. Did this chapter in any way influence your thinking on the marriage commitment? _____ If yes, in what way has your thinking about the commitment changed?

_____

_____

_____

_____

_____

CHAPTER II

1. In what ways might a Christian worldview of marriage differ from a secular worldview of marriage?

_____

_____

_____

_____

_____

2. How might these differences affect the way you approach the marriage relationship?

_____

_____

_____

_____

_____

3. A healthy marriage is dependent upon _____ and the effort _____ put into the relationship.

4. What three characteristics most attracted you to your fiancé/spouse?

_____

_____

_____

_____

_____

5. What do you think might be the flip side of those characteristics or traits?

_____

_____

_____

_____

_____

6. Happiness in marriage depends on both partners contributing equally to the marriage. True _____ False _____

CHAPTER III

1. In entering into a marriage it is wise to have a "backup plan" in case things don't work out. T_____ F_____

2. Why did you answer the above question as you did?

_____

_____

_____

_____

3. When problems arise in your marriage relationship, whom, if anyone, could you rely on for sound advice?

_____

_____

_____

4. If you listed anyone above, why do you feel they would provide sound advice?

_____

_____

_____

_____

5. Who benefits from divorce?

_____

_____

_____

CHAPTER IV

1. Love can be both an _____ and a _____ .

2. In marriage it is more important that love be a decision of the will than an _____.

3. Why do you feel the above statement is true? Give reasons for your answer.

_____

_____

_____

_____

4. The Bible instructs women to _____ their husbands, and husbands to _____ their wives.

5. Does being equally yoked apply only to Christians? Yes ___ No ___

6. Give a reason for your answer.

_____

_____

_____

_____

7. Name some things that might cause couples to grow apart over time.

_____

_____

_____

_____

_____

8. If you died today and God asked you why He should let you in heaven, how would you answer Him?

_____

_____

_____

_____

9. Can you give a Bible verse to support your answer?

_____

_____

_____

_____

CHAPTER V

1. Do you feel honesty is important to a relationship? Yes __ No __

2. Give a reason for your belief.

_____

_____

_____

_____

3. Infidelity always ends in divorce? T ____ F ____

4. The root of jealousy is a lack of _____.

5. Do you feel your relationship would be strong enough to survive if you discovered your partner had an affair? Explain.

_____

_____

_____

CHAPTER VI

1. Would you say you are a good _____ , fair _____ , or poor _____ communicator?

2. Would your fiancé/spouse agree with you? Y ___ N ____

3. Name as many of the eighteen rules of engagement as you can.

_____

_____

_____

_____

_____

_____

_____

_____

_____

_____

4. What communication skill from this chapter do you feel you might be able to best employ?

_____

_____

_____

_____

5. List some factors that contribute to miscommunication.

_____

_____

_____

_____

6. Would people say you are a better listener _____ or talker _____?

7. Are you and your fiancé/spouse comfortable in the deep end of the communication pool, as described in this chapter? Yes _____ No _____

8. Would you say you accept criticism graciously _____ , could use some work, or "don't ask" _____?

9. Are you more apt to retreat from a problem or confront it?

_____

10. What was the most important thing you will take from this chapter?

_____

_____

_____

_____

11. How do you think this information might help you in your communication with others?

_____

_____

_____

CHAPTER VII

1. Not enough money might really be a case of _____.

2. Are you able to clearly distinguish between wants, needs, and desires?

Yes _____ No _____

3. List a want, a need, and a desire you have.

_____

_____

_____

_____

_____

CHAPTER VIII

1. When criticizing, it is important to separate the _____ from the _____ .

2. One of the principles listed in this chapter is: "Interact: Growth comes out of _____. A refusal to _____ is a refusal to _____ in a relationship."

3. What do you think the author means by, "Never waste a good argument"?

_____

_____

_____

5. Arguments are always destructive and should be avoided at all costs. T ____ F ____

CHAPTER IX

1. Name the two types of expectations, and give an example of each.

_____

_____

_____

_____

2. Why is it dangerous to make assumptions?

_____

_____

_____

_____

3. Jumping to conclusions is closely related to making _____.

4. To assign a motive is to pretend to _____ someone

else's _____.

CHAPTER X

1. In a family, traditional roles should always be assumed. T _____ F _____

2. What do think is meant by the Bible verse that says, "The husband is

the head of his wife as Christ is the head of the church"?

_____

_____

_____

_____

_____

3. In a marriage, the husband should always handle the finances.

T _____ F _____

CHAPTER XI

1. What do you feel are some of the key issues that should be reviewed

when taking a family history, and why?

_____

_____

_____

_____

_____

2. Why is it important for couples to establish boundaries?

_____

_____

_____

_____

CHAPTER XII

1. Statistics have shown that sexual relations before marriage improve the chances for having a fulfilling relationship. T _____ F _____

2. Sex in marriage should be discussed openly by the couple.

T _____ F _____

3. Sex was a part of God's plan for the marriage relationship.

T ___ F ___ Explain: _____

_____

_____

_____

4. It is important for couples to pay attention to their physical condition as well as their personal cleanliness to help assure a successful and healthy sexual relationship. T __ F __

CHAPTER XIII

1. When experiencing problems in a relationship, it is best to wait and give them time to resolve themselves before seeking help.

T _____ F _____

2. Where abuse exists (physical, mental, verbal, or substance) separation—not divorce—may be an advisable course of action.

T _____ F _____

3. Therapy is always expensive and takes a great deal of time.

T _____ F _____

4. Not all who counsel are qualified to counsel. T _____ F _____

5. While parents and friends may give advice, they often lack objectivity. T _____ F _____

ANSWER KEY FOR REVIEW QUESTIONS

Chapter I
Q 1 - Subjective
Q 2 - Subjective
Q 3 - Subjective

Chapter II
Q 1 - Subjective
Q 2 - Subjective
Q 3 - me, I
Q 4 - Subjective
Q 5 - Subjective
Q 6 - False

Chapter III
Q 1 - False
Q 2 - Subjective
Q 3 - Subjective
Q 4 - Subjective
Q 5 - No one but the lawyers

Chapter IV
Q 1 - emotion, choice/decision
Q 2 - emotion
Q 3 - Subjective
Q 4 - respect, love
Q 5 - No
Q 6 - Subjective
Q 7 - careers, relationships, education, or interests
Q 8 - Jesus died on the cross for my sins that I might have eternal life, or I have confessed (or asked) Jesus to be Lord of my life, or I believe Jesus died on the cross for my sins, or words to that effect.
Q 9 - Examples: John 3:16; Romans 10:9–10; John 14:6; Ephesians 2:8; John 1:12

Chapter V
Q 1 - Yes
Q 2 - Subjective

Q 3 - False
Q 4 - trust
Q 5 - Subjective

Chapter VI
Q 1 - Subjective
Q 2 - Subjective
Q 3 - Rules of Engagement:

1. Actions speak louder than words. Often we send mixed messages when our nonverbal message is contrary to our verbal message.
2. Define what is important and stress it. Define what is unimportant and deemphasize it or ignore it.
3. Communicate in ways that show respect for the other person's worth as a human being. Avoid beginning statements with absolutes, such as "You never …"
4. Be clear and specific in your communication. Avoid vagueness.
5. Be realistic and reasonable in your statements. Avoid exaggeration and sentences that begin with, "You always …"
6. Test all your assumptions verbally by asking if they are accurate. Avoid acting until this is done.
7. Recognize that each event can be seen from various points of view. Do not assume others see everything just as you do or they should see them exactly as you do.
8. Recognize that your close friends and family members are experts on you and your behavior. 8. 8. Avoid the tendency to deny their observations about you.
9. Recognize that disagreement can be a meaningful form of communication. Avoid destructive arguments.   ·
10. Be honest and open about your feelings and viewpoints. Bring up all significant points, even if you are afraid doing so will disturb another person. Speak the truth in love. Avoid sullen silence.
11. Do not put down and/or manipulate the other person with tactics such as ridicule, interrupting, name calling, changing the subject, bullying, blaming, bugging, sarcasm, criticism, pouting, inducing guilt, etc. Avoid the one-upmanship game—it is simply a controlling behavior.
12. Be more concerned about how your communication affects others than about what you intended. Avoid becoming bitter if you are misunderstood. Miscommunication results in misunderstandings. Always strive for clarity. If you sense you have been misunderstood, restate your communication using different words.

13. Accept all feelings and try to understand why others feel and act as they do. Understand feelings cannot be denied, and avoid the tendency to say, "You shouldn't feel like that."
14. Be tactful, considerate, and courteous. Avoid taking advantage of the other person's feelings.
15. Ask appropriate questions and listen carefully. Avoid preaching or lecturing.
16. Do not use excuses. Avoid falling for the excuses of others.
17. Speak kindly, politely, and softly. Avoid nagging, yelling, or whining.
18. Recognize the value of humor and seriousness. Avoid destructive teasing.

Q 4 - Subjective
Q 5 - mishearing, hard of hearing, poor listening, a lack of communication skills, differing use of language
Q 6 - Subjective
Q 7 - Subjective
Q 8 - Subjective
Q 9 - Subjective
Q 10 - Subjective
Q 11 - Subjective

Chapter VII
Q 1 - too much spending
Q 2 - Subjective
Q 3 - Subjective

Chapter VIII
Q 1 - behavior, person
Q 2 - conflict, interact or engage, grow
Q 3 - Subjective
Q 4 - False

Chapter IX
Q 1 - The two types of expectations are realistic and unrealistic. The explanation is subjective.
Q 2 - Subjective
Q 3 - assumptions
Q 4 - know, mind

Chapter X
Q 1 - False

Q 2 - Subjective
Q 3 - False

Chapter XI
Q 1 - Subjective
Q 2 - There are a number of reasons that couples need to establish boundaries. Perhaps the most important reason among them is that doing so anticipates and thus prevents future problems. Establishing boundaries also helps couples to maintain healthy and respectful relationships with friends and family.

Chapter XII
Q 1 - False
Q 2 - True
Q 3 - True; Explanation subjective.
Q 4 - True

Chapter XIII
Q 1 - False
Q 2 - True
Q 3 - False
Q 4 - True
Q 5 - True

BIBLIOGRAPHY

• Alcorn, Randy. *The Treasure Principle*. Multnomah, 2001.

• Barker, Kenneth L., ed. *NIV Study Bible* (New International Version). Zondervan, 1973, 1978, 1984, 1985.

• Blanchard, Kenneth, and Spencer Johnson. *The One Minute Manager*. Harper Collins, 2003.

• Boehl, David, Brent Nelson, and Lloyd Shadrack. *Preparing For Marriage*. Gospel Light, 1997.

• Boone, Wellington. *Your Wife Is Not Your Momma: How You Can Have Heaven in Your Home*. Doubleday, 1999.

• Burkett, Larry. *How to Manage Your Money*. Moody Press, 1991.

• Burkett, Larry. *Your Finances in Changing Times*. Moody Press, 1993.

• Carty, Jay. *Playing with Fire: Do Nice People Really Go to Hell?* Multnomah, 1992.

• Chapman, Gary. *The Five Love Languages: How to Express Heartfelt Commitment to Your Mate*. Northfield Publishing, 2004.

• Christensen, Monty, and Roberta L. Kehle. *70 x 7 and Beyond: Mystery of the Second Chance*. Impact Publishing, 1998.

• Cloud, Henry, and John Townsend. *Boundaries*. Zondervan, 1992.

• Cloud, Henry. *Changes That Heal*. Zondervan, 1992.

• Collins, Gary. *Christian Counseling*. Word Publishing, 1988.

• Colson, Chuck, and Harold Fickett. *The Good Life*. Tyndale House, 2005.

• Cornell, Laurel L. *I Do: Portraits From Our Journey Workbook*. Family Research Council, 2001.

• Cowan, Connell, and Melvyn Kinder. *Women Men Love, Women Men Leave: What Makes Men Want to Commit?* Clarkson N. Potter, 1987.

• Crabb, Larry. *The Marriage Builders: A Blueprint for Couples & Counselors*. Zondervan, 1992.

• Dahrens, Stephen. *Tools For The Shepherd*. Pastoral Support Ministries, 1988.

• De Shazer, Stephen. *Keys to Solution in Brief Therapy*. W.W. Norton & Co., 1985.

• Dungy, Tony. *Quiet Strength: The Principles, Practices, & Priorities of a Winning Life*. Tyndale, 2008.

• Eggerichs, Emerson. *Love & Respect Respect: The Love She Most Desires; The Respect He Desperately Needs*. Thomas Nelson, 2004.

• Goldberg, Herbert, and Irene Goldberg. *Family Therapy: An Overview*. Brooks/Cole, 1996.

• Gottman, John. *The Marriage Clinic: A Scientifically Based Marriage Therapy*. W.W. Norton & Co, 1999.

• Gray, John. *Men Are From Mars, Women Are From Venus: A Practical Guide for Improving Communication and Getting What You Want in Your Relationships*. Harper Collins, 1992.

• Huckabee, Mike, and John Perry. *Character Makes a Difference: Where I'm From, Where I've Been, and What I Believe*. B&H Books, 2007. (Originally published as Character is the Issue. B&H Books, 1997.)

• Kendall, R.T. *Total Forgiveness*. Charisma House, 1984.

• Markman, Howard J., Scott M. Stanley, and Susan L. Blumberg. *Fighting For Your Marriage: Positive Steps for Preventing Divorce and Preserving a Lasting Love*. Jossey-Bass, 1994.

• Parrott, Les, and Leslie Parrott. *Saving Your Marriage Before It Starts: Seven Questions to Ask Before (and After) You Marry*. Zondervan, 2006.

• Peterson, Eugene H. *The Message*. NavPress. 2002.

• Roever, Dave, and Kathy Koch. *Scarred*. Roever Communications, 1995.

• Sell, Charles M. *Family Ministry: Family Life Through the Church*. Zondervan, 1995.

• Vernick, Leslie. *The Emotionally Destructive Relationship: Seeing It, Stopping It, Surviving It*. Harvest House, 2007.

• ———. "Emotionally Destructive Relationships." *Christian Counseling Today*, American Association of Christian Counselors, 2008.

• Vine, W.E., Merrill F. Unger, and William White, Jr. *Vine's Expository Dictionary Of Biblical Words*. Thomas Nelson Publishers, 1985.

• Wahlroos, Sven. *Family Communication*. McGraw Hill, 1995.

• Weiner-Davis, Michele. *Divorce Busting: A Step-by-Step Approach to Making Your Marriage Loving Again*. Simon & Schuster, 1992.

OTHER RESOURCES MENTIONED IN THIS BOOK

American Association of Christian Counselors

American Heritage Dictionary

"Attitude" by Charles Swindoll

Book of Common Prayer

Crown Financial Ministries, P.O. Box 100, Gainesville, GA 30503-0100; phone: 800.722.1976; Web site: www.crown.org/

eHarmony's Web site: www.eharmony.com

Family Research Council, 801 G Street, NW, Washington, D.C. 20001; phone: (800) 225-4008; Web site: frc.org

Fireproof (movie)

"Meta Model" by John Grinder and Richard Bandler

National Association of Nouthetic Counselors

National Center for Health Statistics

Talmud, Hebrew book

Webster's Encyclopedic Dictionary